T0129224

AN UNCONVENTIONAL
LOVE LETTER
TO THE LGBTQ COMMUNITY

Jessica is extremely transparent about her journey in finding the love and acceptance of God in her life. Her personal story shows God is always looking beyond the labels of society, the stereotypes of culture and reaching straight to the heart of who we are by His love.

—Star Funk, Worship Pastor, The Family Church

I have personally witnessed her transformation first hand. In this book she tells the real life story of the pain of sin and the beauty of finding a relationship with God. Jessica has gone from a young lady seeking help to a person who has ministered freedom to many. Whether you read her book or have her share her powerful ministry, you will be deeply touched!!

—John Brady, Senior Pastor, The Family Church

An Unconventional Love Letter to the LGBTQ Community is bold, raw, real, powerful and full of love. This book has the power to break down the barriers between the LGBTQ community and the church.

—Eli Lara, New Life Family Ministries

AN UNCONVENTIONAL
LOVE LETTER
TO THE LGBTQ COMMUNITY

REDEFINING LOVE. EXPOSING THE TRUE ENEMY.
MY JOURNEY TO FREEDOM

Jessica A. Newsome

WESTBOW
PRESS®
A DIVISION OF THOMAS NELSON
& ZONDERVAN

WestBow Press books may be ordered through booksellers or by contacting:

WestBow Press
A Division of Thomas Nelson & Zondervan
1663 Liberty Drive
Bloomington, IN 47403
www.westbowpress.com
1 (866) 928-1240

ISBN: 978-1-5127-8899-0 (sc)
ISBN: 978-1-5127-8898-3 (hc)
ISBN: 978-1-5127-8900-3 (e)

Library of Congress Control Number: 2017908059

Print information available on the last page.

WestBow Press rev. date: 6/15/2017

ACKNOWLEDGMENTS

First and foremost, I am thankful for my parents.

To my mother who has stood by me through many ups and downs, I am eternally grateful. Despite our past, my mother is a loving and phenomenal woman. I have come to realize that our own past hurts, often causes us to unintentionally hurt others. Pain and lack of forgiveness that are not healed are like festering wounds that continue to deepen in our hearts and lives, producing ripples that affect how we interact in current relationships. I do not harbor any resentment toward my mother. In fact, I know that she did the best she could with what she had. I love her more than all the sand on the beach and stars in the sky. She has taught me many invaluable lessons in life and has made me a stronger woman. I believe that God is restoring our relationship daily.

To my father, thank you for putting up with all of my shenanigans. Although we did not see eye to eye during my adolescent and teen years, you always did what you thought was best. As I strayed down the wrong path and failed miserably in school, you made sure that I graduated from high school and went to college. In spite of my persistent pushback, you remained diligent in getting me back on the right path.

To Karen Crews Crump, thank you for the time you've spent editing the several drafts of this book. I truly appreciate your hard work and dedication in seeing that this book was ready to send to various publishing companies.

To the First Baptist Church of Glenarden and Rising Star Missionary Baptist Church, thank you for unknowingly planting seeds that were so instrumental in breaking down the barriers between God and me. Your pastors and congregations will forever have a special place in my heart.

To The Family Church, thank you. I have never seen a group of people show the unconditional love of Christ through their actions as each of you has. From the day God told me to step foot into your church, I was never the same. You not only opened your doors, you opened your hearts to me, allowing me to grow spiritually through your many discipleship classes while God continued to do a deep work within my mind and heart. Through serving in ministry, God showed me my destiny. Thank you for allowing me to develop my gift within the walls of your church.

To the pastors of The Family Church, thank you. As the world changes, you remain steadfast in your convictions while radiating the fruit of the Spirit. Never have I seen Christ followers love unconditionally those who are lost without expecting an immediate eradication from sin. You are truly loving, patient and kind; a beacon of hope for the Rio Grande Valley. I have learned many life transforming lessons from each of you that continue to play a part in my daily growth as a Christian.

To the board of directors of Love at the Cross, Inc., and prayer partners, thank you for standing in agreement with the mission of this ministry. I am pleased to serve alongside each of you as we continue this journey together.

To those who've walked with and guided me through the early stages of this journey—Nakima, Kim, Star, Denee, PJ, Miss.T, Colin, Stephiana, Eli—thank you (if I have forgotten anyone, my apologies). I would not be where I am today had it not been for your guidance and help as I left the LGBTQ lifestyle. "Where there is no guidance, a people falls, but in an abundance of counselors there is safety" (Prov. 11:14, ESV). To all the individuals who donated toward the publication of this book, thank you. Your contributions are appreciated and immensely valued. *Luke 6:38* (ESV) says, "Give, and it will be given to you. Good measure, pressed down, shaken together, running over, will be put into your lap. For with the measure you use it will be measured back to you." Your investment has and will continue to be used to spread the Good News of deliverance through Jesus Christ throughout our lost and broken world.

CONTENTS

INTRODUCTION

To have a desire to know God while at the same time genuinely loving someone with all my heart, who happens to be of the same sex, tore me apart inside for many years. Trying to figure out where one stands in Christ's eyes, as well as in a homophobic society, can, and often does, lead to depression as well as suicidal thoughts and actions. I know many who were/are a part of the LGBTQ (lesbian, gay, bisexual, transgender, queer) community who have these struggles.

If you had asked me a few years ago, I would have sworn that I was born homosexual, and there was no changing it. I didn't choose to be homosexual, and I couldn't help being attracted to women. My thought was, I can't change it, neither can a pastor, and certainly not God.

I was a modern-day Saul before he became Paul. I boldly used the Bible to justify homosexuality and would debate until I was blue in the face with anyone who opposed "God's truth" or, in other words, opposed my way of thinking and understanding. In my mind, Jesus affirmed loving, Christ-centered homosexual relationships. But one day, God's love invaded my heart, and everything changed.

Many debate what the Bible says about homosexuality, stringently proclaiming their opinions of how God views the topic. Over the years, I have learned that we can read all the books we want and listen to all the debates we choose, but as my good friend Phil Pray once said, "There is only one winner in a theological debate, and that's Satan."

To the LGBTQ, I apologize for how many Christians have treated you. I've been there, received the ugly blows to the heart, and I completely understand. But know this: in spite of the actions of unloving Christians and homosexual bashing protesters, Jesus loves you to the moon and back. God knew you before you knew yourself, before your parents knew you were coming into this world. He has an everlasting love for you that you can never fully understand. Although the world is harsh and ugly, God knows the heartache, and the rejection you've endured from those you love, as well as from the world around you. Whatever you've been through that has scarred and hurt you, know that it wasn't God's doing. We each have free will, and some choose to use theirs for evil. You may have been on the receiving end of that evil, and for that, I am truly sorry.

Setting aside the debates and confusion pertaining to homosexuality and the Bible, each human being must decide, on his/her own, whether or not to follow Christ. This is a personal decision and choice. If you're feeling a desire to get to know Christ and find out what He's truly about, come as you are. Many of us have been told that we must change our outer appearances before we step foot in a church, or we may *feel* that we must because of the uncomfortable glares we receive by church folks. Know that this is not God's attitude toward us. Come as you are. Come as a transgender woman or man, a homosexual taking his/her partner and children to church, and let God invade your heart. I humbly apologize for the Christians who act so unlike our Christ Jesus. If we can push past the opposition of those who don't know our struggles and our hearts, we will come face-to-face with a God who is compassionate, loving, forgiving, and who is a life-changer.

We have become so good at masking the hurt, frustration, confusion, and rejection we feel on the inside in order to tell ourselves that we're fine, and that we don't need this Christianity version of religion. The reality is we all need God. He is the One Who created us, who knows us and has a plan so perfect for our lives that it surpasses all under- standing. No partying, sex, alcohol, drugs, or friends can satisfy the seemingly unquenchable longings in our hearts. Only God can fill those voids. We don't get cleaned up and then come to Christ; we come to Christ and allow Him to clean us up. Those of us who have allowed God to work this process in our lives have found a freedom that we never thought truly existed.

An Unconventional Love Letter to the LGBTQ Community is not a book written to condemn the LGBTQ community. It is quite the opposite. It is a book that recounts my personal journey to freedom and uncovers the main ingredient that brings a person to Christ: love. Love bridges the gap between the great divide that we, Christians and Non-Christians, have created—the gap of homophobia, hate, confusion, hurt, deception, and lies. This book also unveils the spiritual warfare that entraps and entangles those struggling with homosexuality, shedding light on the true enemy, Satan himself. Throughout each phase of my life, I will shed light on the "behind the scenes activity," that is, the spiritual warfare we endure on a daily basis (where Satan wars for our souls).

1 Love

Love is patient and kind; love does not envy or boast; it is not arrogant or rude. It does not insist on its own way; it is not irritable or resentful; it does not rejoice at wrongdoing, but rejoices with the truth. Love bears all things, believes all things, hopes all things, and endures all things.

—1 Corinthians 13:4–7 (ESV)

Many in the body of Christ have strayed from one of the most important characteristics of our Father: *love*. One person's hate and condemnation will never bring another to a place of genuine repentance and desire for God. Too often, this approach is used in an attempt to do just that, and it doesn't work. Treating people as outsiders, or lesser than oneself because they are different, is not Christ-like.

What about the woman at the well (John 4)? Not only did the Jews look down on her because she was a Samaritan, she was also an outcast because she had been married five times and was living with a man who was not her husband. What did Jesus do when He encountered this woman? He showed her love. In spite of her wrong thinking and sinful life, He offered her something that would finally quench her thirst, filling her with wholeness, genuine love, and salvation through Christ Jesus. He showed her a new way that would lead to true happiness, fulfillment, and an eternity in Heaven.

What about Rahab (Joshua 2)? She was a prostitute and everyone knew it, but God looked past her sins and saw her moldable heart. Jesus had mercy on the lost and hurting. He met them right where they were. It was those who were in desperate need who came to Jesus—messed up, sinful, confused, and lost—and He healed them.

It is in those moments of crying out to Jesus that the blinders Satan has placed on our eyes begin to fall away. In the movie *The Matrix,* Keanu Reeves's character Neo was given a choice: he could take one pill and wake up to everything being just the way it was before he met the individuals offering him freedom, and his world would go on exactly as he had perceived it before he was offered the truth or reality. But he could also choose the alternate and *wake up.* He would become aware that the world, which he had perceived to be reality, was in fact, a false reality that forces beyond his current comprehension wanted him to believe was truth. If he chose to *wake up,* life would never be the same. This is what it's like to walk with Jesus. If we choose to follow Him, believing in our hearts and professing with our lips that He is the Savior and Lord over our lives, He begins the process of opening our eyes to the truth, and life as we know it is forever changed.

Satan has done a good job of blinding the eyes of the world so they see only Satan's reality.

> Satan, who is the god of this world, has blinded the minds of those who don't believe. They are unable to see the glorious light of the Good News. They don't understand this message about the glory of Christ, who is the exact likeness of God. (2 Cor. 4:4, NLT)

We as Christians need to understand that the battle is not between the LGBTQ community and us, but the battle is with Satan. If people are blinded by the devil, how is our getting frustrated and angry with them going to solve anything? It is not we who change others, but God alone changes the hearts of unbelievers and opens their eyes to the truth. We are simply the people who plant and water (lovingly spreading the Word of God). God is the only One Who gives the increase (gives the individual a personal revelation of Christ) (1 Cor. 3:7).

I spent years hiding the fact that I had an attraction to females while I quietly searched for the love and acceptance I heard so much about from Christians, but found none. I did, however, see a lot of religion: the judgmental, self-centered, self-righteous, gossiping, fake kind of Christians who would repulse any outsider. Can you imagine how the conversation would have gone if I had told them I was attracted to women? I thought if they found out, I would be stoned, or they would immediately lay hands on me and try to cast out demons!

Most, if not all of us, in the LGBTQ community have at some point quietly searched for the antidote to our same sex attractions. Oftentimes, guilt and shame prevented many of us from speaking loud enough for someone to hear. Too often, the thought of finding someone who could walk with us through this journey or just finding someone who could relate to us seemed unattainable. Know that God's love never varies; He cannot love us any more or any less. His love for us remains unchanged whether we are living in sin or walking in the footsteps of His son Jesus.

Change does not come overnight. I spent many years beating myself up over the fact that my change didn't come quickly. I now know that it's a process, and through that process, God's love is steadfast, unwavering, loyal. Even when we fall or mess up, He loves us just the same.

2 The War

As an adult, I've always said that I was born a homosexual.
From my elementary school days, I remember having same-sex
attractions. It wasn't something I asked or searched for.

I couldn't tolerate—no, I hated it when people tried to reason
me into thinking there was some root cause to my being a lesbian. I
actually still support the premise that I was born that way. Why? We
were all born into sin. The moment Adam and Eve ate of the fruit
from the forbidden tree of knowledge of good and evil, they gave
authority over the earth to Satan. Sin was ushered into the world,
and from that day forward, a war wages on the inside of us—a war
between flesh and spirit. Make no mistake; we do not simply live
in the physical realm (the world as perceived with our five senses).
We also live in a spiritual realm, which goes unnoticed by many.
We are first and foremost spiritual beings. We aren't simply flesh
and bones, but a three-part being (I will explain this later). In the
spiritual realm, there are two kingdoms: the kingdom of darkness
where Satan rules and the kingdom of light, where we are invited
to live with God. The choice is ours. Our flesh often craves and
desires things that would harm or hinder us spiritually. At this
moment, many of you are probably wondering, *What is she talking
about? Spirit? Satan? I've never seen demons or angels. If they exist,
then where are they?*

Good question. I could say something cliché like, "Just because you don't see it, doesn't mean it's not there." Although this statement is true, it is not enough to sway the unbeliever. I will attempt to make this more understandable in a moment. First let's explain the Spirit.

When I talk about one's spirit, I mean the core essence of a human being. A human is a three-part being, consisting of body (flesh), soul (mind, will, emotions), and spirit. We can see the flesh, but we cannot see the soul or spirit. Before Adam and Eve sinned in the Garden of Eden, they were spiritually alive. To be spiritually alive is to have the Spirit of God (Holy Spirit) within. When Adam and Eve sinned, the Spirit of God left them.

> But of the tree of the knowledge of good and evil you shall not eat, for in the day that you eat of it you shall surely die. (*Gen. 2:17*, ESV)

When God says, "You will surely die," He was referring to a spiritual death. Because they ate of the tree of knowledge of good and evil, we all now are born into a body and have a soul, but we are spiritually dead. The only way to become spiritually alive is to receive Jesus (Who paid the penalty for sins when He died on the Cross) into our lives. Since all humans are spiritually dead, God begins tugging at our hearts. He wants to transform us by giving us spiritual life so we can live fulfilling lives. God wants to equip us to live victoriously over the enemy who aims to destroy us spiritually, emotionally, and physically.

Jesus said in John 10:10 (NIV), "The thief comes only to steal and kill and destroy; I have come that they may have life, and have it to the full."

Concerning angels and demons, I can't conjure up a few to show you, but what I have learned is through firsthand experience and through the experiences of others. The Bible has much to say about both angels and demons. People are hesitant to talk about *things that go bump in the night* because they don't want to look crazy, or they fear others won't understand. Hosts of people have experienced the supernatural realm. I will discuss this in more depth in another chapter.

The supernatural realm is just as real as the physical realm in which we live. Some experience the demonic within the supernatural realm while high on drugs. Others experience it because they have opened their spirits to Satan.

The good news is that Christians have authority over all the powers of the forces of evil in the supernatural realm.

> For though we walk in the flesh, we are not waging war according to the flesh. For the weapons of our warfare are not of the flesh but have divine power to destroy strongholds [Satan's]. (2 Cor. 10:3–4, ESV)

> For by Him [Christ] all things were created, in heaven and on earth, visible and invisible, whether thrones or dominions or rulers or authorities—all things were created through Him and for Him. (*Col. 1:16*, ESV)

If we could place a world within a world, this would be my example of the supernatural realm. It's right here, all around us, but we don't necessarily see it. There is constant activity in the supernatural realm, and it's just as real as the activity we can see, feel, and touch in the physical realm.

Satan wants people to believe that he, God, and the supernatural realm don't exist. If he can convince us that these are not real, then we have no need for God. We will cling to the belief system that we are in control of our lives; we are the gods of our lives. If Satan can accomplish this, then destroying us spiritually, emotionally, and physically is not that difficult. While we are living on this earth, Satan will unceasingly wage war for our souls. We feel this tension in the areas of the flesh that is sinful in nature (desiring to follow Satan) and the soul, which encompasses the mind, will, and emotions. Satan is constantly deceiving our souls and flesh, and we so often fall victim to his tactics. Below are a few hypothetical examples of the battle between flesh and spirit.

Example:

Drugs alter the state of mind and are often used as an escape or are used to numb emotional or psychological pain. The user becomes dependent on the drugs, which leads to addiction. How can a person fulfill the first and greatest Commandment of the Bible, "you shall love the Lord your God with all your heart, with all your soul, and with all your mind," (Matt. 22:37esv) if one's mind is altered or clouded by drugs?

The war that ensues: The desire to stop using drugs verses the flesh craving the drugs and ultimately becoming addicted to them.

Example:

Movies/shows that are sexually provocative in nature put desires, whether the producers have done it intentionally or unintentionally, into our minds and hearts. Many say, "What's the problem with watching a certain movie? It's just a movie!"

The problem is if we don't guard our minds and hearts (our spirits), we allow sin and Satan to have rule over these areas of our lives. Can we go to strip clubs and think that the nature of that environment won't rub off on us? Can we watch pornography and think it will not pull us into Satan's trap? Don't we understand that we soon crave the type of sex we see in the videos? Over time, hunger for more exotic ways of "pleasure" increases and spirals out of control, pushing one into an unreal world of demands for "sexual fulfillment."

The war that ensues: Our flesh says it's okay to do these things. It's not hurting or harming me or anyone else. Our spirits battle to *not* commit adultery, but because we have fed our minds with the women/men who portray "desirable individuals" in movies or porn, we lust. Because of porn or masturbation, we battle being content sexually with our spouses.

> Guard your heart above all else, for it determines the
> course of your life. (Prov. 4:23, NLT)

When we guard our hearts, we are protecting ourselves. Protecting us from what? From being deceived. The devil is subtle when enticing people to follow him. We must be vigilant—continuously growing in our relationship with Christ; otherwise, we fall for Satan's deceits.

I love this quote that has been quoted by many individuals:

> Watch your thoughts; they become your words.
> Watch your words; they become your actions; watch
> your actions; they become your character; watch
> your character; it becomes your destiny.

From the moment we are placed on this earth, the devil is at war in an attempt to destroy us. If Satan keeps us feeling rejected, guilty, or ashamed, he has us, and he will do his best to not let us go.

3 My Story: Rejection

Beginnings to Age Eleven

only remember bits and pieces of my childhood. Because of the traumatic incidences I endured, my tiny mind blocked out so many things. These are the account of what I do remember.

Since my earliest memories, I can recount feelings of loneliness, rejection, and being unloved by those who mattered most to me. I often tippy-toed around the temperaments of my mother and felt unloved by my father. My father was a hardworking man and provided *everything* I needed, except what I needed most— love. I could say that he showed me love by providing for me, but he wasn't speaking my love language. I needed more than material things.

He was always so busy working or arguing with my mother that I felt as though I was put on the back burner. During the fighting and arguing, which seemed to fill the major part of my childhood, I became a recluse in my room. My bedroom was my little piece of heaven. In my room I was safe, although I knew that at any given moment, an explosion of anger or frustration from my mother could invade and overpower my already timid nature. Living on the edge of fear, I constantly monitored the moods of my parents and based my actions according to their temperaments. I feared drawing attention to myself. As strange as it may seem, I began to find comfort in rejection—it was my "normal." For fear of being yelled at or not understood, I learned at an extremely young age to mask my hurt feelings and cover them with a facade of happiness. It was as if my feelings were at times just an inconvenience.

Often I felt I had to be the mediator between my parents; I had to keep them calm so that tempers wouldn't flare. At times I felt I had won the victory of averting the predictable storm between the two, but at other times, I became the punching bag.

On one occasion, I remember my father telling me that I should throw away my mother's cigarettes because they could kill her. So I walked to the front door and threw them outside as far as I could—approximately five feet from the door—and they landed in a thorn bush. The next thing I remember is my mother on a rampage trying to find her cigarettes. I knew if I told her while she was angry that I had thrown them away because "I didn't want her to die," I would soon have her crouching down to my level, screaming and yelling at me like a drill sergeant at a new recruit. I was terrified at what I knew was going to happen very soon. When she figured out what I had done, I received just that. She yelled at me to go get them from the thorn bushes. I remember the thorns scratching and pricking my flesh as I worked my little arm through them to retrieve her cigarettes. Finally, after getting the cigarettes and handing them to her, she cursed me out for what I had done then stormed off. She left me there by the front door, shaking in fear, hurt, and alone. I quickly headed to my room—my safe place.

One weekend my father, mother, and I were traveling back from North Carolina when they got into a huge argument. While they screamed at each other and began shoving one another in the front seat of the car, I remained terrified, yet silent, in the backseat for fear of making the situation worse. If I said anything, the wrath would quickly be splashed in my direction with no filter on the lips of my mother. A few minutes later, my father pulled over onto the side of the highway, and my mother and I got out of the car. As my dad drove off, my mother began crying uncontrollably, and then we started walking down the side of the highway while cars zoomed past us. After a while a car stopped, picked us up, and took us to a store where we waited for someone to come get us and take us to our house.

Hours later, we finally got home, and I went upstairs to my room. As I passed my father's room, the door was cracked open about three inches, and I saw him lying in the bed eating popcorn and watching television. Never once did he tell me he was sorry for leaving me on the side of the highway. I felt like trash—something that could be thrown out of a car window without a second thought.

Scenes like this, as well as my observing the addiction to drugs, alcohol, and sexual promiscuity, were not uncommon during my childhood. My perception of love was skewed. One moment I was verbally and physically abused, the next, I was held and told, "I love you more than anything." What a mind trip for a small child!

A normal parent-child relationship was pretty much nonexistent between my dad and me. I remember a few occasions when we spent time together—about the same with my mother—but not enough to properly articulate.

During all of the hurt, I am grateful for the times that I visited my aunt and uncle's house and saw what a family was supposed to look like. I remember watching how they interacted with one another. When they seemed to be irritated with one another, they didn't verbally or physically lash out at each other. I was amazed. I would (and still to this day on occasion) often become tense, worried, and scared when adults peacefully argued, thinking it was just a matter of time before things would explode out of control. When I went to my aunt and uncle's house, I was smothered with hugs and kisses from my aunt. I never felt safer than when my aunt would wrap me in her arms and tell me how much she loved me while consoling me. I loved being close to her. She always seemed to melt my problems away.

I remember running from my aunt's house to my grandmother and grandfather's house across the street. There was no place like my grandmother's house. She was the best at everything—hugs, kisses, and especially cooking. I loved to get into her bed, wrap myself in her blue comforter and smell it. I loved the smell of her perfume. Throughout my childhood, Grandmother's house was my ultimate heaven-on-earth. I spent many days running back and forth between the two houses, creating unforgettable memories with my cousins.

At a very young age, I fell into a downward spiral of depression. I didn't recognize it as such because it was life as I knew it. It was my normal. I did, however, find a bit of comfort in the few childhood relationships I had. During elementary school, a friend introduced me to "playing house." At first I was taken aback by the closeness involved in the game, but later I found comfort in her affection. This is my first recollection of having same-sex attractions. Around the same time, I remember having the biggest crush on a babysitter who at times picked me up from the bus stop after school. She had chocolate-brown skin and long black hair, and I loved to be close to her and look at her. I often wondered what it would be like to kiss her the way I kissed my friend when playing house.

Although my father and grandparents took me to church on a fairly consistent basis, I felt a separation between God and me. The God of the Bible, the Hero, the Knight in shining armor, was nonexistent in my life. I didn't feel loved, safe, or happy. I didn't see God in my life. I thought, *If my own parents don't love me or care, why should God?*

Because of the lack of proper love shown to me by those closest to me, it was hard for me to let anyone else love me. Thoughts of being manipulated or disappointed crowded out any hope of something genuine, so I continued to isolate myself in my bedroom and bottle up my feelings.

Spiritual Warfare

Rejection causes people to cling to those who WILL accept them.

What is the devil's purpose?

- To destroy the relationship between God and man
- To keep us in bondage (sin, depression, fear, addiction) so we don't grow in Christ
- To make sure we do not understand our identity in Christ
- To ensure we do not fulfill our God-given purpose here on earth

We all desire to fit in and to be accepted. When we constantly feel rejected by those closest to us or by a specific group of people, many may experience social isolation, which can negatively impact a person's emotional and psychological health. Depression, worry, low self-esteem, acting out, rebellion, thoughts of being unworthy of love, etc., begin to consume one's life.

If Satan can make us feel unlovable, if he can make us think that we are not good enough to be accepted, then it is easy for him to destroy any relationship between God and us. Many feel that God, being so perfect, looks down upon us. Because we may feel God is displeased with us and could never love us, we automatically disconnect ourselves from ever discovering who He truly is.

Why do we do this? Because it's easier to walk away from something or someone rather than to stick around and possibly be hurt again. I speak with many individuals who have a difficult time letting God love them because of this very thing. If we could grasp the fact that yes, we are imperfect, that we will always mess up, but God knows this and loves us anyway, we could break free from Satan's grasp and allow our perfect God to show us that He loves our imperfect selves. This then will allow Him to change those imperfect areas in our lives. If we could grasp that God is not like our parents, no matter how good or bad they are, that He is infinitely better than they are, that He won't let us down, and that we can trust Him, our lives will change greatly.

Too many times, because of continued rejection, we are left with unhealed wounds that keep being reopened before they have time to heal. As these wounds become more and more infected, we settle for who *will* accept us just as we are. Many times we find solace in individuals with the same wounds as ours. "Birds of a feather flock together."

God placed every person on earth for a purpose. It is up to us to seek God and find that purpose; however, we can choose to walk through life without Him. Christ *loves* each of us unconditionally. No matter who we are, or what we've done, He wants to have a relationship with us and show us a life worth living. The devil will do anything to keep us thinking that we do not deserve Christ's love and acceptance because he knows that if we discover the truths of the Bible, it will set us free (John 8:32). When we know this truth, and believe it in our hearts, we begin to come to the realization that in God, we have power over all the works of the devil. We have God-given authority to defeat Satan's plans for our lives.

4 My Story: Depression/ Betrayal

Age: Eleven to Seventeen

fter my parents separated, my mother and I moved not too far from where we were living with my father. My daily life continued to revolve around the attitudes and temperaments of my mother, and I worked at becoming as invisible as possible. Although my father paid child support, due to financial problems, we moved several times throughout the years. As a single parent with a daughter to care for, the stress level was high for my mother, and she chose to numb her pain with alcohol or drugs.

Once during my middle-school years, we were evicted from our townhouse. I came home to find all our stuff on the sidewalk, and a scavenger was picking through my belongings. It was terribly embarrassing for me. I quickly tried to cover it up with the best excuses I could think of because one of my mother's rules was, "We keep our business to ourselves and we always stick together."

Life with my mother was volatile, unstable and unpredictable. I was continuously pushed aside and ignored because, as she constantly reminded me, she had "problems of her own." Oftentimes, she just didn't want to be bothered with me.

I continued to retreat inwardly, masking my feelings with

smiles and laughter, so no one was alerted to my mother's many shortcomings. It hardly ever worked. I thought if I appeared happy, it would be less likely that people would confront my mother or question my welfare and make her angry. The less stressed she was, the less likely I was going to receive a spew of anger and abuse.

One time a close relative asked me if I wanted to live with their family. I desperately wanted to say yes. It would have been a dream come true. To be far away from my mother and that toxic environment would have been a blessing. But all I could think of was how my mother would react. She would make not only my life unbearable the moment she found out, but their lives as well. As early as elementary school, I lived a life of trying to save everyone from her. It felt like she was always arguing with family and picking fights when they didn't see things her way. She seemed to make everyone's life around her miserable. So I said, "No, I'm fine."

Talk about feeling dead on the inside. As much as I hated my life, I couldn't bear someone else having to deal with her, having to feel the way I felt. I wanted everyone to be happy, and if I had to be unhappy for that to happen, it was a cross I was willing to bear.

There were times when we would spend the night at her boyfriend's house. It didn't matter if it was a school night or not. I was to be quiet, unnoticed, and in need of nothing. I was never to interrupt them. Even as a child I knew what they were doing.

Oftentimes I would find her pornographic videos or naked pictures of boyfriends in boxes under her bed in her bedroom. I'm not sure if I was intrigued or indifferent to the pornographic videos. The first time I took an unlabeled videotape from under her bed and put it in the VCR to see what it was, I gaped as the actors engaged in sexual activity. I was captivated and soon absorbed any pornographic material I could find. As I kept myself locked away in my room, I spent countless hours a day watching pornography, submerging myself in lustful desires.

As a kid, I often made meals for myself. At times there would be minimal food in the house, and since I couldn't cook full meals, I'd often make sugar sandwiches, or eat whatever junk food there was around the house (pickles, candy, mac and cheese), or walk to the nearby grocery store with my best friend where we would purchase TV dinners and heat them up. I remember at times telling my mother that I was hungry, and she would fuss and yell through her bedroom door at me because I was bothering her, then tell me to find something to eat.

When I got to middle school, I had more freedom to hang out with friends. Most of the time my mother wanted my friends and me close by, rather than at someone else's house, so she could keep an eye on us as we played. This was perfect because, more likely than not, she was locked away in her bedroom.

Often I found her marijuana stashes around the house. It smelled gross, so I never wanted to try it. My friends and I did, however, find her liquor and cigarette butts, and we'd take sips and smoke the little bit of cigarette that was left. We often went to my male friend's house down the street, and he would get us cigarettes. We would socialize and hang out, doing whatever we pleased. I began smoking at age eleven, and my desire for pornographic material increased rapidly. My friends and I would often play sexually suggestive games.

As a child I remember playing with a Ouija board with a friend. When my mother found out, she was furious. She told me to throw the game out, which I did. I immediately walked to the dumpster in the middle of the townhouse complex and threw it inside. The next day my mother opened the closet door in the hallway and saw the board on the top shelf. She, of course, thought I had ignored her request and asked why I didn't throw the board away. I told her several times that I did, and after a while we both knew there was something demonic about the situation.

I knew she believed me. She mentioned several times throughout my growing-up years about her experiences with ghosts and such that would leave me with an eerie feeling. My friends and I also experimented with things like levitation, playing "Bloody Mary" in the mirror, hypnotism, horoscopes, etc. My favorite type of movie was demonic or horror related. I was intrigued by demonic activity, yet at the same time, terrified.

My hatred for life, my parents, and myself began to deepen.

Middle school was the beginning of extremely dark days for me. I had so much garbage in my life that it was becoming harder to keep a smile on my face, pretending that everything was okay. The hatred I had for my mother became overwhelming. I never knew what side of her would show. She could be sad and crying about how no one loves her and everyone is against her, then switch to being verbally and physically abusive, then move on to drowning her sorrows in alcohol or drugs. I was sick of the sight of her. I often contemplated how I would kill her or myself. Life was not worth living, and I did not understand how a "loving" God could allow a child to go through all that I was enduring. I thought, "No one cares about me, so why should I care about anyone else or myself!"

From the age of eleven, I had a very dark view of life. I had a diary that would have probably put me in a behavioral health center if anyone had read it. I wrote murderous poems, and 90 percent of my diary entries were covered in tears, sadness, hate, and anger. I felt betrayed by the ones who were supposed to love me, and I felt that I was left in this world to fend for myself. My parents were good at ignoring their own personal issues just to appease the public (church or family) as well as remaining blinded to my rapid downward spiral.

I thought, "If no one wanted me, then why didn't they just abort me when they had the chance?" I felt that this would have been the nicest and most considerate thing they could have done. My mother once told me that she tried to make the marriage work between my dad and her, and she had me, thinking it would save their marriage. She may not have meant it the way I understood it, but her words cut deeply into my heart. I was a save-the-marriage baby that didn't work.

Sometime between eight and ninth grade, my father informed me that he was taking my mother to court for custody of me. Up to that point, I was just spending most weekends with him. I thought a lot about with whom I should live, which was a no-brainer. I could no longer take the verbal and physical abuse from my mother and was failing in school. My mother had no idea that I was going to tell the judge that day that I wanted to live with my father. I was terrified. I knew the repercussions of going against my mother.

The day of the hearing, the judge asked me to step inside of his chambers. He sat me down and asked me if I wanted to live with my mother or father. I was terrified of the consequences of her finding out that I wanted to live with my father. I sat in the chair in silence. The judge asked questions to try to get me to open up. He pulled out a stuffed animal in the shape of a dog. I love dogs. He told me that I could have it. I was glad for the present, yet on the inside I was still scared to death. He proceeded to ask me again if I would like to live with my mother, and I was silent. He then asked if I would like to live with my father. I barely said yes and gave a slight head nod. He asked a few more questions and that was it. I left his personal chambers and waited in the hallway with my aunt, near the courtroom where my parents were.

Moments later, like a flood, I heard yelling, screaming, and crying. My heart began to pound against my chest. My hands trembled as my mother came out of the courtroom chambers being held and consoled by her boyfriend. I will never forget what she said the moment she saw me. Being held back and guided away from me by her boyfriend, she yelled and cursed at me. "I never want to see your face again, and I mean it! You're dead to me!", is just part of the string of words directed to me. Later, when my father took me to her townhouse to get my belongings, I found all my clothes thrown about in the yard. My mother did not talk to me the whole summer. I really thought I was never going to hear from her again, and it hurt me that she couldn't understand that living with her was not healthy. It's crazy to think that a child can have the right mind to make such an adult decision and then watch the parent throw a temper tantrum.

In the years to come, I was to learn a lifelong lesson. Most of the time I had to be the parent, while my mother was the child. I couldn't change her. Hearing phrases like, "I never want to talk to you again; you're dead to me," would be like a continuous stab in a wound that never healed. The wounds from my mother are still there, even as I write this book, but God is working His healing process.

During high school I began drinking heavily. I guzzled beer and took shots effortlessly. Drinking was the perfect escape. The reality of life disappeared, and the world temporarily became enjoyable. As much as I hated my mother's lifestyle, here I was, doing exactly what she had done before me.

In tenth grade, while living with my father, I began attending a new school and had to make new friends and create a new life. I became close friends with a girl I will call Leah. Our friendship quickly developed into a romantic relationship. We spent lots of time together at her house, locked away in her room. I was becoming extremely comfortable with my feelings toward females and having sexual relationships with them. I quickly found myself falling in love with her and wanting nothing else but to spend time with her. Not negating the genuine feelings I had for Leah, as I look back, I believe what I experienced was more lust than love. Every chance I had, I'd try to get her to her bed and push her out of her comfort zone sexually.

I was pretty much always the aggressor when it came to guiding her toward sexual activities. Years of watching porn had created lustful desires that seemed to spiral out of control and made me pretty bold in obtaining what I desired from other girls. She was not the first female I was sexually active with, but she was the first one I "loved" romantically. Since I was not yet proclaiming my sexuality to the world, and she didn't want anyone to know, we kept everything quiet. I'd often get her attention through the door of her classroom, and she would meet me in the bathroom where I would steal as many kisses from her as I could before she had to go back to class. While with other friends in the hallways or cafeteria, we would exchange knowing glances. Sex was always on my mind. It took over my life. And I liked it.

Living a double life, I went every Sunday and Wednesday with my father or grandmother to church. I played the flute in the instrumental ensemble during services and sang in the choir. All of this forced, of course. I was there because I had to be, but I quickly found myself eyeing other females my age as well as grown women. I soon began creating friendships with girls at church, having ulterior motives that were anything but godly. I wanted more than friendships, and I had learned how to manipulate other females to get what was most important to me—sex, which was my twisted view of love and affection.

Several times during high school, I tried to stop being attracted to females because part of me wanted to be normal like everyone else, but my flesh spoke way louder than the God I knew of but was not connected with.

I tried dating popular guys, but that was extremely short-lived. They may have been attractive, but every time they wanted to get close to me or kiss me, I was repulsed. The thought of a boy wanting to kiss me or have sex with me made me sick to my stomach. Throughout high school, while attempting to become attracted to guys, I continued secretly having sporadic sexual encounters and relationships with girls. I tried playing the role of a straight girl for a while but eventually gave it up.

I wanted help, but I was afraid to ask. I heard people at church say all the time that God could fix anything. I had the conviction deep down inside that told me homosexuality was wrong, and it often plagued my mind. Yet all I saw were Christians on TV with picket signs telling homosexuals they were going to hell, church folks who cringed with disgust at the thought of homosexuality, or horrible stories of what happened when Christians did admit they had same-sex attractions. These scenarios caused me not to seek help because of the drama and expectations for immediate change placed upon homosexuals by the Christian community. I had enough problems as it was.

For several years during high school, I saw a mental health professional. The anger, frustration, self-hate, and depression seemed to spill over into every area of my life. My father took me every Wednesday to group counseling. I hated going and often put up a fight.

My father and I didn't get along, nor could we hold a civil conversation without yelling. I couldn't open up to him because of his old-school ways of handling things. He was more of a "straighten up, fly right, and get it together" kind of man. I needed for him to listen and understand the things I was going through when I tried to explain why I was so angry and hurt. But he had a "deal with it and move on" mentality. Admitting he was wrong was usually far from his vocabulary. He was more like a school principal rather than a loving, understanding father.

Don't get me wrong, I know now that he showed love the best way he knew how—by providing for me, which he did very well. But as a teenage girl, my needs went much deeper than that. We bumped heads constantly and often avoided each other. He remarried when I was in tenth grade, and his relationship with his new wife was just one more blow to my wounded spirit. I couldn't understand how he could be so kind, loving, and attentive to someone else but not listen to and understand me. This made me angrier, and my hatred for him and my new stepmother grew as time went on.

When I visited my mother on weekends, it was the party house. My friends would come over and we'd drink and smoke. My mother didn't have a problem with the drinking, but we hid the smoking from her. Although my life seemed to be filled with excitement on the outside, I was miserable on the inside.

I began cutting myself as a way to escape from my evolving problems. Many people don't understand cutters, and as a kid, I really couldn't articulate it myself. I was so used to being an inconvenience to my parents, feeling like I was a mistake, feeling unloved, and constantly being verbally and physically abused that I found comfort in treating myself just as badly. I cut my wrists and thighs as punishment for things like opening myself up just to get hurt by others. My thought process was, "You should have known better, Jessica. *Everyone* will hurt you." Or I would cut simply for existing as a waste of space on this earth.

Inflicting physical pain on myself somehow masked my inward pain. I would feel calm afterward and usually would drift off to sleep after I bandaged my wounds with toilet paper or paper towels. The more blood, the more at ease I felt.

Depression/ Betrayal

If Satan can keep you down, he has permission to keep you.
The enemy walks through dry places

The devil walks through dry places trying to find rest (Luke 11:24, Matt. 12:43). If he can find a dry and barren place, he will make himself comfortable there. What is a dry place? Jesus said He is the Living Water, and whoever drinks of the Living Water will never thirst again. Without Jesus and the life-giving water of the Spirit, our souls are dry and barren places. When we are not walking in the fruit of God's Spirit (love, joy, peace, patience, kindness, goodness, faithfulness, gentleness, self-control), but rather walking in the opposite of it (sadness, confusion, hate, strife, depression, sin, worry, lack of self-control), the devil has an opportunity to wreak havoc in our lives. I'm not saying that as Christians we will never experience these negative feelings. It's quite the opposite; we will have these feelings because we are human, but what we do with them is most important. If we choose to stay in a negative state of mind and refuse to turn to Jesus, the devil will enjoy making an already bad situation worse.

Most children don't know how to surrender their lives to God so that He can help them. That's why it's so important to raise children in godly homes, so they are protected as much as possible from the enemy's assaults. The actions of those around me gave the devil a perfect place to rest.

How was my life a dry place?

1. Finding comfort in same-sex relationships
2. Hating myself and others
3. Cutting
4. Drinking excessively
5. Suicidal thoughts and actions
6. Sexual promiscuity
7. Playing with the Ouija board, participating in witch- craft/occult activities

25

8. Absorbing words of rejection, hatred, disappointment, and disgust spoken over me by those closest to me

Once the devil has us in his trap, he will do anything to keep us there. He desires for us to listen to his lies and stay bound, unable to find freedom from his grip. If we remain in this state for long, we begin to believe the lies of the enemy. What lies has he been telling you? Maybe he's telling you that you will never be free from your sin, that you cannot find happiness if you give up homosexuality. He may be telling you that everyone has given up on you, and there is no use in attempting to be a better person. He will tell you that you're just like your father or mother, that you will never be anything.

Don't let Satan keep you in the chains of your past. We will never achieve our God-given potential in life if we stay stuck in dry places. There is freedom in Christ Jesus.

Spiritual Warfare

The devil desires for us to follow him. If he can't accomplish that, he will attempt to make our lives miserable so we don't follow Jesus.

During my adolescent and teenage years, I had no clue why I was going through such agony in life. I could not grasp the concept that there was a war going on that I couldn't see—a war Satan is waging against the human race to destroy mankind from the inside out (mind, body, and soul). God desires eternal salvation for humanity, and that all be made whole (mind, body, and soul) through Jesus Christ. Trying to understand Satan's deceptive and manipulative tactics he uses to entrap and control individuals via their mindsets was incomprehensible to me during those years.

The Bible says in Ephesians 6: 10–18 (NIV) (The Armor of God):

Finally, be strong in the Lord and in His mighty power. Put on the full armor of God so that you can take your stand against the devil's schemes. For our struggle is not against flesh and blood, but against the rulers, against the authorities, against the powers of this dark world and against the spiritual forces of evil in the heavenly realms. Therefore put on the full armor of God, so that when the day of evil comes, you may be able to stand your ground, and after you have done everything, to stand. Stand firm then, with the belt of truth buckled around your waist, with the breastplate of righteousness in place, and with your feet fitted with the readiness that comes from the gospel of peace. In addition to all this, take up the shield of faith, with which you can extinguish all the flaming arrows of the evil one. Take the helmet of salvation and the sword of the Spirit, which is the word of God. And pray in the Spirit on all occasions with all kinds of prayers and requests. With this in mind, be alert and always keep on praying for all the saints.

Whether we know it or understand it, we are in a war. We can see war being waged in the natural (civil wars, wars over religion or race, etc.), but there is a war going on that few can see. This war is in the supernatural realm. Some Christians have a gift to see and operate in the supernatural realm while others who practice Satanism can do the very same thing. Many under the influence of drugs have seen demons or angels. Others experience seeing shadows walking around in their rooms or experience sleep paralysis that many try to explain away.

Left unarmed and not understanding the power we can have in Christ Jesus, we fall victim to the tactics of the enemy. Once he has us in his grip, he will do his best to keep us there. Too many remain bound by the enemy. They walk around with heavy hearts and overwhelmed minds because of the things attached to them. They walk around with huge backpacks full of depression, suicidal thoughts, and feelings of guilt, shame, confusion or worry. We were never meant to carry these loads through life.

We all know people close to us who still talk about relatives who did them wrong twenty years ago and are still deeply hurt. Because of the hurts and negative feelings, they continue to carry and give pieces of their baggage to others with whom they come in contact. For example, they speak negatively; they teach their children that they should never depend on anyone because everyone will let them down and hurt them. They may drown their pain in alcohol, thus, teaching their children, through example, that these are appropriate ways to deal with their problems. They are unknowingly passing on their baggage to their children. Their children may walk through life not allowing anyone to get close to them, missing out on a fulfilling life in Christ.

God says, "Come to Me, all of you who are weary and carry heavy burdens, and I will give you rest. Take My yoke upon you. Let Me teach you, because I am humble and gentle at heart, and you will find rest for your souls" (Matt. 11:28–29 NLT).

Once we begin to seek Jesus, we begin the process of equipping ourselves against Satan.

The Armor of God

- **Belt of truth buckled around your waist**—Know that the Bible is the truth. There is nothing to be added or taken away from it. Deception through twisting of the Word of God is the enemy's plan.
- **Breastplate of righteousness**—A breastplate protects our vital organs from fatal blows. It is important that we do not let the enemy penetrate our core with lies and accusations about our pasts. We are in right standing with Christ because of our faith, our trust in Him.
- **Feet fitted with the readiness that comes from the Gospel of peace**— Shoes give us solid footing and allow us to put our focus on what lies before us rather than worrying about obstacles thrown in our way by the enemy. Feet now

properly fitted, we can focus on what God has called us to do.

- **Shield of faith**— A shield is used to block the fiery darts of the enemy. Whatever the devil throws at us, we block those darts by declaring in faith what the Word of God says. In so doing, we remain safe from the enemy's attacks.

- **Helmet of salvation**— A helmet protects the most vital part of the body. Any spiritual attack begins in the mind. The devil wants us to doubt, to think negatively, and get our minds off God and His Word.

- **Sword of the Spirit**— The sword is our only offensive weapon. Our weapon is our knowledge of the Bible. If we know the Bible by taking time to study it, along with developing a relationship with God, we can cut through and slice any attack of the enemy because we know the truth.

- **Pray in the Spirit**— Praying in one's native tongue and also in the Spirit are vital. By praying in the Spirit, we are praying in a language that we don't understand, but the Spirit within us intercedes perfectly on our behalf to God. Many times we can only pray for a few minutes in our native language because we don't know what else to say or how to articulate what we are trying to say. But by praying in our prayer language, the Spirit takes over, and we can pray for hours. If you're wondering, "What is she talking about?" don't worry, I will explain this in detail later on in the book.

5 My Story: Delusion/ Illusion

Age: Seventeen to Twenty-three

One morning while visiting my mother for a weekend, I was awakened by the sounds of sexual activity. Freaking out and disgusted by each sound and sexually suggestive remark, I quickly got dressed and headed toward the door to leave the house. Having to pass by her room, I glanced at the cracked open door and was sickened by what I saw. I wish I could erase it from my memory because even to this day, horrible images and sounds from that experience will randomly assault my mind.

When I confronted her later on, I was told, "This is my house…"

Angry, yet not surprised, I shrugged it off.

Many events throughout my life gave me my rational for how I chose to live my life. Everyone else seemed to do what he/she wanted while justifying bad behavior, so I decided to do the same. I developed the attitude that respect was earned, not given. I felt that my parents did nothing to earn my respect, so I never gave it to them. I had one life, and I intended to live it the way I wanted, and nobody was going to stop me.

In my junior/senior year of high school, I was becoming comfortable in my newfound sexuality and started seriously dating females. I had "come out" to my friends. At first I told them that I was bisexual because I was not ready to admit to anyone or to myself that I was a full-out lesbian. My friends were uncomfortable at first, but over a period of time, they accepted my lifestyle.

Living in my father's house was like living in a prison, but when I went to my mother's house on weekends, I had, for the most part, freedom to do what I wanted. My mother was more like a sister at this point in my life. Sometimes we would get along, and she would let my friends and me have our fun, but at other times she would curse us out for whatever reason she saw fit. Throughout my late teenage years, I blatantly disrespected her and crossed the line on several occasions because of my disdain for her and her lifestyle. Her actions provided plenty of fuel for my hate towards her.

My parents began noticing things that led them to believe I was having "inappropriate" relationships with females. Looking back now, I was never good at hiding notes or the fact that I always wanted to be around a specific female friend, spending extended amounts of time on the phone with her or at her house. I didn't have a cell phone, so using the house phone made things incredibly obvious. Trying to be quiet, so I didn't awaken my father and stepmother, I'd make late-night calls.

I couldn't force myself to be someone I wasn't, and I was tired of trying. My heart wanted what it wanted, and I couldn't keep ignoring it. I was tired of waiting on a God that couldn't hear me. My trying to hide my sexuality all this time led me to suicidal thoughts and actions. I knew my lifestyle was sinful in the eyes of God, and I was old enough to understand the Bible, knowing that it clearly states that homosexuality is wrong, but I couldn't change me. I didn't think God could either. The war inside me was overwhelming and excruciating. I would often try my best to divert my thoughts away from these convictions or block them out with friends, alcohol, partying, etc., but nothing could fill that void within me.

If I turned on the TV, I would see the LGBTQ movement for equality—same sex couples fighting for their rights and wanting to simply be treated like everyone else. I saw the hurt and heartache in their eyes and lives. I saw the hate toward the homosexual community from those who called themselves Christians. Picket signs condemned homosexuals while picketers screamed obscenities towards them.

I was repelled by the hatred and began to empathize with those who were hurting and who were being judged by the very religion I claimed as my own. This was the breaking point.

This was my thinking: we live in a free world. I shouldn't be forced to live within the restraints of Christianity. I don't have to stay in the box my parents and their religion placed me in. The very people who are supposed to love me treat me horribly, and I continue to be their little puppet they use and abuse.

I came to the conclusion that the God I claimed to follow was just like them: harsh, unloving, critical, and showed no remorse for what He allowed "His children" to go through. Nor was He sympathetic to the fact that I *could not* turn off the gay and that I was literally dying from the inside out.

I was tired of living for my parents, and I was done living for God. While pretending to be who my parents and God wanted me to be, it was becoming impossible to keep how I felt bottled up inside. The anger, hatred, frustration, and hurt began spewing out through my attitude and my increasing defiance. I remember one time when my mother thought that I was having an inappropriate relationship with another female, which I was, she came to the girl's house. When my friend's mom opened the door, my mom came into the house and started beating on me as I came up the basement steps and continued to pound on me as we left the house.

During my senior year, my parents found out that I was having relationships with other females. Fearing the consequences, I tried my best to explain it away and lie about it, and it sort of worked. When it was time to graduate from high school and head to college, I thought, *This is the perfect time to tell them I'm a lesbian. I'm leaving for college and there's nothing they can do about it now.*

Coming out was just like I had imagined: painful and hurtful. I expected nothing less than their best verbal, physical, and mental abuse. My mother was disgusted, but my father pretended I had never spoken of it and chose to simply ignore it for as long as he could.

Before I left for college, I had the last conversation I would have with God for a very long time. I told God that I was tired of the overwhelming conviction that homosexuality was wrong. I was done with my parents, and I was done with Him. I told Him to leave me alone and basically, go hang out with Satan in Hades. That was it.

The convicting presence of the Holy Spirit quickly left. Entering college, I had no idea what I was getting myself into. So much freedom! Finally, I could be me, and no one would hold me back and try to control me. The first thing I noticed about the university was that it seemed to have a large population of homosexuals. I couldn't believe it. I was a kid in a candy store. So many flavors, and I could have as much candy as I desired. Between graduating high school and the end of my two years in graduate school, I had been with over twenty-one individuals, including two guys.

One of my first male friends during my freshman year of college soon became a best friend of mine. Out of sexual curiosity, we had sex. Having never been with a guy, I thought this might be the cure to my lesbianism. I remembered my mother asking me, "How can you say you don't like guys if you've never tried it?" So I did just that. I tried it. This experience with my best friend lasted all of four seconds. At the sight of his genitals, I wanted to gag. What girl would allow *that* near them? I attempted this twice in my life. I thought that if I had sex with a guy, then I would discover that I enjoyed it, and I would have succeeded in my effort to be normal.

Total fail. I hated it and wondered why I wasted my time. I felt like I had just sold my body, and for free. It's crazy, with all the women I slept with, I never had that feeling. The few relationships, one-night stands, or friends with benefits never fazed me. After the failed attempts at sex with men, I was seriously finished. It was gross. I was disappointed that I even wasted my time with something so repulsive.

At the end of my freshman year, I got kicked out because of failing grades. Extensive partying took its toll. I crafted a well-written sob story about how my parents actions were affecting my school work and that the stress at home caused me to have failing grades, and was allowed back in the following semester. I became a professional liar and used the skill when needed.

Sometime during my second year in college, a female friend and I met a local police officer who was on duty near the party spots where my friends and I hung out in Washington, DC. I was interested in getting to know him because my goal was to become a police officer. We talked for a few minutes and exchanged numbers. Sometime later, my friend and I took him up on his offer to come to his house. His apartment became a new hangout place for us in the city, and because we were too young to buy liquor, he would buy if for us. He had police gear, which we played with, and he had a hot tub. My girlfriend at the time didn't like the fact that I hung out with him, but I did it anyway. He was thirty-five and we were around nineteen.

One evening, while a female friend and I were at his house, we got in his hot tub and got drunk as usual. I got out first, leaving them behind because the mix of alcohol and the temperature of the hot tub was becoming overwhelming. I migrated down the hall to check out one of the rooms in his house. The room I stumbled into had a sex swing and a few other sex toys.

I remember the guy following me into the room, and then, to my horror, he raped me. Several times I told him to stop, but he didn't, and I was too intoxicated to do much about it. I tried to push him away but couldn't and eventually gave in. When he finished, he walked out of the room like nothing had happened. In shock and too intoxicated to gather complete thoughts and feelings, I went to find my friend and found her passed out on his bed. He had passed out right next to her. I desperately wanted to leave, but I knew neither of us was in any shape to drive. As I sat there on the side of the bed next to her, my initial thought was, *This is all my fault. I'm nineteen, and I somehow think that a thirty-five-year-old police officer wants to just hang out and give underage girls free alcohol. How could I be so stupid?* I didn't want to leave her in the bed with him by herself, so I sat on the floor by her side of the bed, in disbelief at what just happened. When I sobered up enough, I woke her up and we left immediately.

Driving back, I didn't tell her what happened, and after dropping her off, I drove to my girlfriend's house and began telling her the whole sordid story. Crying as I detailed the horrifying events of the evening, to my amazement, she yelled at me instead of consoling me. She was furious that I had gone over there when she had told me not to. She made me feel like all that had happened was to be expected and that it was my fault. Honestly, I felt the same way, but I never asked to be taken advantage of. I couldn't believe that she was making me feel worse about an already horrible and traumatic event, but it did confirm to me that this was entirely my fault.

I went to my doctor not too long after the incident to get checked out. As I told her what had happened, I was extremely nervous and uncomfortable. When the results of my lab work came in, I sat in nervous expectancy. I never thought I would be put in a situation where I would be in fear of being pregnant or contracting an STD (sexually transmitted disease). Thank God I was not pregnant, but I did end up getting an STD from him. I was given pills and was extremely grateful that what I had could be cured. It was not something that I would have to live with for the rest of my life.

Although I felt like God had abandoned me, I realize now that throughout my life He was there—waiting silently in the background. He wasn't there to override my bad choices, but I do believe He diverted major consequences for some of my actions. I am thankful that He was there when I should have gotten several DUIs. He intervened when I could have killed someone when I got in the driver's seat while intoxicated. He was there when I could have been taken advantage of sexually as I hung out and partied with people whose moral integrity was questionable. He was there time after time when I was so close to committing suicide. He was there when I should have gotten alcohol poisoning and died. Silently He waited in the background, knowing what I had the potential to become, knowing who I would become, and He protected me as much as I would allow Him to. In spite of my cursing Him for the parents He had given me and for the deck I had been dealt, He had patience with me while He silently worked behind the scenes and waited for me to come to Him. He had an eternal love for me in spite of myself.

College for me was a modern-day Sodom and Gomorrah. It was a blur of alcohol-induced stupors, parties that involved whipped cream and cherries, black lights, strip clubs, gay clubs, gay pride parades, tattoo parties, and even engaging in sex while others watched and much more. I remember joking around with my friends as we talked about "turning" straight girls. It was a game of cat and mouse. The more straight girls we could turn, especially the good girls, the more verbal accolades we'd receive.

I enjoyed every part of my little Las Vegas. It gratified every increasingly lustful desire I had. When morning came around, we cleaned up our act and got busy being the good studious students that we were. My circle of friends had high aspirations, mostly to get their doctorates, which they all achieved. It was normal, however, to party in whatever way we chose in the evening then make a 180 degree turnaround when daylight came.

For a time during undergrad, I was a part of an on- campus organization that promoted the equality of the LGBTQ community. When it came to the homosexual agenda, we wanted equality and to not be treated like outcasts by homophobic individuals, which seemed to be the status of the world we lived in.

Because knowledge of God was instilled in my heart while growing up, the seeds had been planted but were going nowhere. There was nothing I could do to uproot what I already knew about God. After a while I did a little research on what homosexual Christians believed and dove headfirst into this type of thinking. I quickly adapted to the gay-Christian viewpoint and beliefs. It's crazy now to think that I called myself a Christian, claiming to love and be a follower of Jesus Christ and yet indulging deeply in things anything but godly. I seriously saw nothing wrong with my lifestyle. I was totally blinded from the truth.

Spiritual Blindness

We refuse to wear masks and play games. We don't maneuver and manipulate behind the scenes. And we don't twist God's Word to suit ourselves. Rather, we keep everything we do and say out in the open, the whole truth on display, so that those who want to can see and judge for themselves in the presence of God. If our Message is obscure to anyone, it's not because we're holding back in any way. No, it's because these other people are looking or going the wrong way and refuse to give it serious attention. All they have eyes for is the fashionable god of darkness. They think he can give them what they want, and that they won't have to bother believing a Truth they can't see. They're stone-blind to the day- spring brightness of the Message that shines with Christ, Who gives us the best picture of God we'll ever get. (2 Cor. 4:2–4, MSG)

When we refuse to understand or follow the Bible, we are directly or indirectly choosing to follow the god of this world, which is Satan. The moment we begin to follow Satan, he begins to blind us to the truth, and instead of following God and His Word, we follow what *we think* is right. In essence, we become our own gods, and nothing could make Satan happier because we are doing exactly what Adam and Eve did in the Garden. They ate of the fruit of the Tree of Knowledge when the serpent said, "…when you eat from the tree your eyes will be opened, and you will be like God…" In other words, "You won't need God; you can be your own God."

Throughout college I struggled deeply with suicidal thoughts and actions: cutting, depression, self-hatred, etc. I was hurting on the inside and didn't understand why. No girlfriend could fill the void within me. No amount of alcohol, number of friends or college degrees could make those feelings disappear.

Only my childhood best friend, Elaine, who attended the same university as I, knew about my problems and the extent of them. We'd known each other since fifth grade, and if anyone knew me, it was this girl. One time as I was attempting to drown my problems in alcohol and cutting, she walked in on me. I don't remember much of what happened; I was too drunk. What she saw, though, scared her enough that she called my mother, but apparently my mother dismissed it or just didn't care. I was embarrassed at being caught, and I kept telling my friend to leave, but she wouldn't. I never wanted anyone to witness that part of my life. It was supposed to be a secret. I was skilled at bandaging my wounds and hiding the cuts and scars so that no one knew or suspected anything.

Any time a relationship would go bad for me, I didn't know what to do with the feelings of rejection. I couldn't understand why someone would cheat on me or didn't want to be with me anymore. The rejection and pain of being dumped or cheated on wounded me deeply. Because I couldn't do something as simple as keeping a relationship together, I punished myself. Out came the bottle or the blade. Sometimes both.

I thought something I was doing was causing them to run. Or maybe it was because I didn't have the Barbie-doll- type body or I was not as pretty as the next girl or I didn't dress to impress like other women did. Because of the need to be what others desired, I became a chameleon. I also bought what I could for them to please them. I bent over backward and dropped everything for whomever I was dating, but I still got dumped.

My life was fun at times, but definitely out of control. When the police knocked on my door the third time I got arrested, it didn't even faze me. My thought was, *Oh well, what can you do about it?* My life was in a major downward spiral.

During graduate school I began to genuinely seek God on my own for the first time. I considered myself a homosexual Christian and had even written a twenty-five-page term paper entitled, *Homosexuality and the Bible*, in which I used the Bible to justify homosexuality. I convinced other homosexuals who were confused that traditional Christianity was wrong. I had shaped God to fit my lifestyle. Amidst the craziness of my life, I attempted going to church. I went a few times to a small, lively, upbeat AME (African Methodist Episcopal) Church off campus. I enjoyed attending services and felt a sense of relief while I was there, but I also felt conviction about how I was living my life. With that being said, attending church services

39

during this time of my life was short-lived. I was not ready to give up the only life I knew.

Delusion/Illusion

> For the time is coming when people will not endure sound teaching, but having itching ears they will accumulate for themselves teachers to suit their own passions, and will turn away from listening to the truth and wander off into myths. (2 Tim. 4:3–4 ESV)

Conviction is God's way of letting us know that what we are doing, or about to do, is wrong and will steer us off the path He has set before us, if we continue to ignore His warnings. What does conviction look like? Conviction is that thing on the inside of us that says don't steal, don't drink and drive, don't try that drug. When we go to throw our trash away, and it falls on the floor instead of into the trashcan, conviction says, "Don't leave it there; pick it up and put it in the trash." It's an inner sensor (the Holy Spirit) that taps on the conscience and urges us to behave differently.

Take a look at your life. When have you felt convicted about doing something but chose to do it anyway? What happens when you ignore the conviction you feel? If you constantly ignore it, you become numb to God's voice in your life.

Many times we try in our own strength to "do right." Many times we fail. Why? It's because we are sinful by nature. When homosexuals try to "not be gay," using their own will power, they will fail every time. They may be able to fake it on the outside, but I guarantee there is a battle going on in the inside.

I thought I was giving God a chance when as a teenager I asked Him to "make me straight," but I didn't want to have to change *me* in order for it to happen. I didn't want to have to change other areas of my life. I wanted Him to take away my sexual desire for females, but I didn't want to dedicate time to reading the Bible and actually paying attention and applying what I learned in church. I didn't want to stop drinking, change my friends, or give up other aspects of my life that I thoroughly enjoyed. It took about ten more years before I understood how God works in our lives. He is not my genie to Whom I could bark orders then sit back and wait for Him to do His job.

We have to understand that God is an all-or-nothing package. If we want what He has to offer, we have to give Him every part of our lives.

How can He heal us if we don't give Him the opportunity to work in all areas? Giving our lives totally to God is the most rewarding thing we Christians can do. It brings true freedom and happiness. By submitting our lives to Jesus, He frees us from the bondage, hurt and pain that we've been carrying, and He begins the process of change. But it won't happen until we totally surrender our lives to Him.

Thinking that God couldn't hear me or change me, as a teenager I decided that Christianity just didn't work. Satan never comes up with anything new—he fed me lies, misconceptions, and false beliefs about Christianity just as he has done with generations of people before me. From there I began searching for something to believe in. Everybody believes in something, whether it's religion, atheism, or rationalizing a belief in nothing.

Spiritual Warfare

Satan's Battlefield

One of the most noticeable battlefields between the supernatural and the natural is in the mind. Although we cannot see what is going on in the supernatural realm, we do know what's going on in our minds. Have you ever noticed the struggle between doing what is right and doing what is wrong? Or how it is second nature for humans to attempt to justify wrong behavior or wrong thinking? Or consider the thoughts that randomly go through our minds— perverse, sick, extremely immoral thoughts—that we would never admit to a soul were there. Satan and his demons whisper things in our ears hoping the thoughts will take root and create anger and bitterness or desire. He wants us to act on them, and in doing so, start us down a path to destruction (John 10:10—"The thief comes only to steal, kill, and destroy...").

Certain movies often give good examples of this. The main character is constantly being influenced by uncontrollable thoughts that seem to appear out of nowhere (feelings of depression, anxiety, thoughts of needing sex right now, suicide, hate, rape, anger, lust). The main characters, not knowing how to get rid of those thoughts, eventually fall victim and indulge in the acts.

Have you ever felt like that? I have. I could be having a perfectly good day when my mind would drift to everything my life lacked. It could be money, relationships, health or whatever the devil whispered in my ear to make me feel dejected. If we decide to listen to the whispers and to give in to the feelings of sadness and wallow in them for a little while, we may become depressed or decide to drown our sorrows in alcohol, partying, sex, or whatever temporarily fills the void within.

If the devil can mess us up in our minds, he can begin to drag us down a path of torment like a snowball gathering speed down a hill. He may use something small from childhood or some negative experience. Then he continuously adds to it through words of negative affirmation, feelings of self-hatred, guilt, insecurities, and the hopeless pursuit of trying to please people, pushing our lives toward destruction. After a while, the snowball picks up speed and gets larger and larger and becomes impossible to stop, regardless of how desperately we try to do so.

We can spend our entire lives trying in our own strength to defeat Satan on this battlefield. Apart from God, it will be exhausting, and even if we succeed in shooing the devil away for a short time, he will come back. Only God can bring complete and lasting victory over Satan in our lives.

Just as important as victory over Satan, we need to understand that we cannot fill the voids that are created in our lives after we have been set free from our pasts. Only God can fill them.

For example, when we've been set free from any stronghold, we need to immediately begin filling ourselves with the Word of God. Otherwise, we give that stronghold a wide-open door of opportunity to come back with a vengeance and take root again. Ultimately we will project any unresolved issues into our personal relationships, onto our children, and eventually they will influence every area of our lives, oftentimes driving us to become bitter. Bitterness left unchecked will take root and choke out the limitless possibilities God has for our lives.

Bitterness left unchecked may create an alcoholic because the person doesn't know how to deal with the trauma of his/her past. It may create atheists because God "wasn't there for them when they cried out in a time of desperate need." Bitterness will prevent people from having healthy relationships because someone close to them once told them that they will never be the woman or man they are desiring to be, and they believe it.

The only way to true freedom for all of us is to give our lives to God. God is love, and when we surrender to Him, He gives us hope, His Word, and these things will transform our minds.

Romans 12:1–2 says that we are to present our bodies and dedicate all of ourselves to God and not be conformed to this world with its superficial values and customs, but be transformed and progressively changed by the renewing of our minds, focusing on godly values and ethical attitudes (found only in the Word of God), so that we may prove for ourselves what is good and acceptable and perfect in His plan and purpose for us. Ephesians 5:26 (ESV) says, that he might sanctify her [us], having cleansed her by the washing of water with the word.

The victory on the battlefield of the mind is only won through the strength of God that comes through a healthy relationship with God based in His Word.

My cousin Tabitha (left), her dog Cody and me (right)

Me and my Aunt

6 My Story: Confusion

Age: Twenty-three to Twenty-four

After two years of graduate school, I dropped out when I received an entry-level position with the federal government, serving at the local airport in Washington, DC. Most of my friends had graduated and either gone off to schools in the south to get their doctorates or had begun working. I was left with few friends nearby.

Soon after I started working, I began dating a girl I had met in the area. After a month or two, we were living together. There was less partying but still a lot of drinking. This relationship with my girlfriend (I will call her Alex) felt like an upgrade from all previous relationships. She had a good job, and from outward appearances, we seemed to be the happy couple. Soon after we began living together, I noticed a few problematic areas in our relationship. Although she seemed perfect on the outside, she was very manipulative and condescending. Every day, my already nonexistent self-esteem was bruised and beaten. Depression, suicidal thoughts, and cutting continued to encompass my emotions and engulf my daily life.

Alex was not comfortable with outwardly portraying her sexuality. And to top it off, she was bisexual. I couldn't stand it. One of the things I said I would never do was to get into a relationship with someone who was bisexual. The thought of my girlfriend talking about sex with a guy made me want to puke. And believe me, she proved me right. She found it humorous that I would get mad or disgusted when she spoke about ex-relationships with men. It made me furious. I spent a lot of time trying to be what she wanted me to be. I was the cooking-and-cleaning housewife by day, then the playboy-bunny girlfriend she desired at night. She was very specific as to what she wanted and liked. I had to cater to her every whim or she would often become cold. She was never satisfied with me just being me.

It's a lose-lose situation attempting to please someone who will never be fulfilled by what you have to offer, no matter how hard you try. Like the rest of us, she had a set of problems of her own that she needed to deal with, and our relationship could never move forward unless she found help for them. Looking back now, I know only God can fix, heal, and fulfill the needs she had.

In an attempt to salvage the relationship, I asked her to come to a church I had heard about. The church was LGBTQ-friendly, and I thought it would be good to check it out. The moment we walked in, I felt uncomfortable, and I know she did as well. There were only a handful of people in the congregation. Although I understood it was an LGBTQ-friendly church, I was unprepared for the fact that all I saw were homosexual couples. Although I claimed to be a homosexual Christian, I *knew* what I had just walked into was wrong. Nothing about the service felt right. My spirit didn't sit well in that place. Alex and I never attended services there again or anywhere else for that matter.

After dating for almost a year, we called it quits. I could no longer put up with the mental and emotional abuse, so I moved into my own apartment. Then a few months later, I moved into my best friend Elaine's parents' house. Elaine had moved back home after school and was on the job hunt. Living with them was fun. I enjoyed the family time we spent with each other, and it was a breath of fresh air to be around and involved in that environment. It took me back to our childhood of just hanging out and having fun. I loved it. I had applied for a federal law enforcement position and was currently in its hiring process. There were several steps I had to complete before being offered the position, so I was spending much of my time preparing for them. To be physically fit, I began working out with a personal trainer and ran several miles every day. Elaine's father cooked healthy food and ran with me. He'd always been like a father to me, and I was grateful for his encouraging me, as well as being my running buddy.

While living at Elaine's house, I had become fed up with the reality of my life. I thought things would have changed when school was over and all of my partying buddies were gone. I assumed that the voids I felt on the inside would disappear after I removed myself from my carefree college lifestyle. Was I ever wrong!

Nothing changed. I seemed to have carried over all my problems into the next chapter of my life. In my mind, without the house parties and clubs, there was no reason to drink alcohol, but I soon realized that I craved alcohol and needed it to have a good time. Cigarettes helped me relax and get through a few hours at a time.

Negative thoughts about my life and myself swirled through my head constantly. Doubts about my future and my competency to live an adult life plagued me. Self- hatred, depression, fear, loneliness, and suicide always had a tenacious grip on me. The one thing I didn't want was to turn out to be an exact replica of my mother, but that was where my life was headed.

Without ever being quenched, my hunger for love and affection raged relentlessly. After each failed relationship, I sank deeper and deeper down Satan's rabbit hole. I knew that if I continued down this path, I was going to commit suicide. Exactly when, I didn't know.

I was fed up with how I felt on the inside. I didn't want to feel like cutting myself every time I couldn't fulfill the needs of my significant other, nor did I want to rely on other people to make me feel good about myself. I wanted to stop hating myself and was tired of the facade I displayed so well in front of others because it was slowly killing me. Depending heavily on alcohol to numb the pain of my life, I was often a very angry drunk.

I needed to start over but didn't know how. I tried every option I could think of to fix the broken pieces of my life and nothing worked. There was, however, one thing I did not try whole-heartedly, and that was life in Jesus.

Confusion

"Then you will call on me and come and pray to me,
and I will listen to you. You will seek me and find me
when you seek me with all your heart. I will be found
by you," declares the Lord, "and will bring you back
from captivity…" (Jer. 29:12–14 NIV)

Jesus came to set the captives free. Until we find freedom in Christ, we are all captives to the enemy's devices. No matter how good a person's life appears to be, at the end of the journey here on earth, he or she will stand before Jesus Christ. Heaven and hell *are* real. We are all bound for one or the other. There is no neutral ground. Our final resting place is decided by how we relate to Jesus.

What do we do when we have exhausted all possible efforts to fix our lives, and ourselves, and we are still in the same mess? Do we accept our seemingly unchangeable circumstances, believing that we have to accept the hand that life has dealt us, and simply try to survive?

For some, suicide becomes the last option. I cannot count all of the times I wanted to end my life. Living with a sick feeling in the pit of my stomach because I simply existed, I often sat, staring blankly at the wall in my bedroom with tears rolling down my face and neck. While listening to music that fueled hatred for myself and for the world I lived in, I cursed my very existence. But I could never do it; I could never push past whatever was keeping from committing suicide. I couldn't drink enough alcohol to get me to take that last step; I didn't have enough guts to end it all. I felt like a joke. I couldn't even muster up the strength to end my life! Why couldn't I do it?

There was always something holding me back, and I knew it was God. I hated the fact that I grew up in church because no matter how much I wanted to commit suicide, I was unsure if I would go to heaven or hell for all of eternity. I didn't know where I stood in the eyes of the Lord. And I knew that as bad as my circumstances may have been, it was nothing compared to an eternity in hell with Satan. The trade off was definitely not worth it.

Everyone is different when it comes to what they consider to be overwhelming circumstances with which to cope. No matter what your threshold for pain and hurt is, your feelings and thoughts *do* matter. You matter to someone, and someone *needs you to live.* If you can't think of anyone, just know that *I* need you to survive, because I know God has so much in store for you. You probably can't even fathom that right now, but it is true. *God wants you to live.* He created you for a reason, although it seems to you that He couldn't care less.

Your *less than desirable* circumstances are not the result of God not caring about you. They are the result of Satan's trying his best to destroy you. What has caused you to survive this long without taking that final step and committing suicide? I believe it is the loving hand of God protecting you until you can find truth.

Although it was the unanswered questions about eternity that kept me from committing suicide, it seemed as though I was holding on to these unanswered questions by a thread and at any time the thread could snap and I would end it all.

Even if you seem to be holding on by a thread, keep holding on. I know what it looks and feels like to be in such a dark place, but there is light at the end of the tunnel, and there *is an end* to that tunnel. Keeping suicidal feelings and thoughts bottled up is not healthy. A good place to start is to find support groups to attend or find a mental health counselor who will work with you, someone you can trust who will encourage you and lift you up. These two things helped me immensely growing up.

When I found myself failing in every attempt to fix my problems on my own, I finally gave Christ a real try. I had spent so many years trying to make God fit my lifestyle and then becoming angry with Him when He didn't bless my mess. So often we tell God to give us a boyfriend or girlfriend, but instead of allowing God to transform us into someone worth dating (fixing our broken pieces), we go out and get into a relationship with someone who is just as broken as we are. Then we get angry and complain to God because the relationship isn't prospering. Or we ask God to take away our desires for alcohol or homosexuality, but we don't allow the process of deliverance in our lives. Attending church, reading the Bible, praying, developing healthy Christ-centered relationships, and letting go of people who hinder our growing in God, are all a part of that deliverance. It's about creating a personal relationship with God—His being number one and your being second.

I would ask God to take away the suicidal thoughts, the cutting, and self-hate. I expected Him to work like a genie and make it vanish. Wrong! How can we expect any deep cut to heal if we don't allow the healing process to start and finish? It takes time, and we can't make it disappear instantly. Any deep wound will look like a deep wound for a while even though it has started the healing process. As a deep cut on the body begins to close gradually, we have to be careful to not tear the new skin that's beginning to cover the wound. If it's ripped, the process has to start over; new skin has to form again. The same is true with our souls. We can't keep doing the same thing, yet expecting different results.

Once the new skin has covered the area, it starts to itch as it continues to heal. God may ask us to give up a few things, which is always uncomfortable. There may be scars left, but scars remind us of the things we've overcome. Just like the healing process in our body, we have to allow God to start a healing process in our spirits. God's healing process is a two-way street that many choose not to navigate. Usually we try everything else before we seriously give God a try. But when we do choose to give Christianity a try and allow God to work within our lives and hearts, we find that we wish we had chosen this avenue a lot sooner. All of the wounds that we allow God to heal leave scars that serve as reminders of God's healing and restoring power. We can show our scars to others, letting them know that there is healing through Jesus Christ.

7 My Story: Acceptance of God

Age: Twenty-five to Twenty-seven

At age twenty-five, I started attending church again, and the first church I went to was a Pentecostal church. I didn't know what that meant, but I soon found out. Everything was good until the altar call. I went up for prayer and everyone was in a straight line from left to right in front of the altar. As the pastor prayed for people, he placed his hands on them, and they fell to the floor like Mike Tyson had knocked them out. Some were on the floor screaming or crying or babbling in a language I had never heard before. I was terrified.

As the pastor worked his way down the line toward me, I didn't know what to expect. Was I going to fall out like everyone else and start speaking gibberish? Was I going to start screaming? If I fell out, would I have some kind of spiritual dream? As the pastor got closer, I started freaking out on the inside, and my heart was pounding. I couldn't even remember why I had come up to the altar. The next thing I knew, the pastor put his hands on me and started praying, then a few moments later he moved to the next person. I stood there wondering what had just happened, or hadn't happened, for that matter. I glanced around and everyone was on the floor except me.

Feeling uncomfortable and out of place, I walked back to my seat, wishing I could disappear. Was I so messed up that God had just passed over me? I never went to that church again.

DISCLAIMER:

There is nothing wrong with a Pentecostal church, and I have nothing against them. Being new to Christianity, I didn't know or understand the gifts of the Holy Spirit and was overwhelmed by what was happening. As I grew in my faith, I better understood the things that seemed questionable at first.

The following week I attended the First Baptist Church of Glenarden in Upper Marlboro, Maryland. The moment I walked in, I felt comfortable. Everyone was very welcoming. The praise and worship was like an earthquake threatening to crumble the walls I had built up between God and me. Tears flowed down my face, but I didn't quite understand why. The worship resonated within my soul as I poured out every broken piece of my heart in tears before God. When Pastor Jenkins delivered the sermon, I soaked up every word as it awakened something inside me that had been sleeping far too long. I knew immediately that I had found my church home.

One Sunday at the end of the sermon, the pastor asked if there was anyone who wanted to receive the free gift of salvation that God offers to each of us through His son Jesus Christ, Who died for all of our sins so that we might be forgiven and receive eternal life. With tears in my eyes, I accepted that free gift. Once I did that, I became a new creation. As soon as I could, I began taking the new-members classes they offered and attending every Bible study and Sunday service. I also decided to get baptized again.

I had been baptized as a child, but I really didn't know the significance or magnitude of that decision. I was so happy. My father and stepmother came and supported me as I gave my life to God. It was then I finally decided to pick up the Bible and read it for myself. In the past, I followed along as pastors would read the Scriptures or lesson for the day, but that was it. Even in college, I derived my thoughts and opinions from sources who claimed to have read the Bible themselves. I agreed or disagreed with their conclusions on major Biblical "hot topics." For the first time ever, I opened my Bible and started at the beginning: Genesis 1:1. From that day, my whole life began to change. During 2008, I spent most of my time working, exercising, or attending church. I still partied a bit, smoked, and drank. By midsummer I had been single and without friends-with-benefits for a few months. One day, as I was taking a walk, I prayed a prayer: "God, please give me a God-fearing woman who is not crazy and full of drama, a woman who loves You and is nice. If You want to add icing on the cake, let her be able to cook as good as my grandmother. Thanks."

Not too long after I prayed that prayer, I met the last girlfriend I would ever have. I will call her, Aaliyah. She was everything I could have asked for. Through her, I saw my many imperfections and shortcomings. She had everything I wanted. She was kind, sweet, patient, loving, and beautiful inside and out, and she had a nine year old daughter who was absolutely perfect. A few months later, the federal position I had applied for became mine, and I had to attend a five-month academy. After completion of basic training, I was permanently stationed in South Texas. Aaliyah and her daughter moved to McAllen, Texas, where I had rented an apartment for the three of us.

Life was good. I was far from the distractions of home and thrown into a new environment. I worked a lot and didn't party much with others. Although I still drank pretty heavily and smoked, I tried to hide these vices from Aaliyah's daughter. I focused on providing for my new family and keeping them happy and loved nothing more than to see my two favorite girls get whatever they wanted. Although Aaliyah was extremely independent, I tried my best to provide everything she needed. I would have given them the world if I could have. I never thought I could love someone else's child the way I loved Aaliyah's daughter. Her daughter was beautiful, very polite, and had an awesome personality. I loved her smile and wanted to give her the moon and stars. She was my little princess.

When I came home from work, I usually had a few beers and smoked a few cigarettes to relax. Because things were going so well during this relationship, depression, suicidal thoughts, cutting, etc., were suppressed, for the most part. Yes, there were ups and downs like in any other relationship, but overall, Aaliyah was the best thing I had ever known; however, I often got myself into trouble with my flirting. All of the years of promiscuous dating had ingrained something in me that I didn't know how to get rid of. Even though I was finally in a decent relationship, I couldn't stop flirting with other people. I loved the attention and had a deep-seated desire for something that Aaliyah couldn't fulfill.

I wanted to change, but I couldn't. I tried my best to keep the negative qualities of my personality at bay, but every now and then they would surface. Often I'd go to the adult novelty shop and buy porn, then hide the stuff in the closet and hope that Aaliyah didn't find it. Even though she always did. When I discovered that I could get porn for free on my phone, I was able to feed the beast that resided within me whenever I wanted. Aaliyah would get so mad at me because I'd sometimes choose porn over her. There was no former partner who could satisfy me the way she did, but it wasn't enough. I learned to be secretive in order to avoid arguments with her.

We found a small church near our house where everyone was very welcoming, and we began attending services. It was obvious we were a couple, but no one ever said anything or alluded to their knowledge of it. That was different for me. I was used to hiding my sexuality and dating relationships from Christians in fear of persecution or ridicule as they stared in dismay. Their eyes always spoke louder than their words. There was so much hate, distain, anger, judgment, and disgust in their eyes. It didn't have to come from their lips for me to notice. The people at this church were not like the average Christians I was used to. They loved us and accepted us into their church family. They would invite us over to their houses for family get-togethers, as well as invite us to local events. Finally I was accepted, flaws and all.

Acceptance of God

> For by grace you have been saved through faith. And this is not your own doing; it is the gift of God, not a result of works, so that no one may boast. (Eph. 2:8–9, ESV)

When we decide to follow Christ, we come to Him as we are: imperfect, broken, messed up, flawed. Too many times, people feel they have to get themselves cleaned up then come to Christ for His approval. That is not the case. God knows all about our imperfections. He knows the horrible things we think and do. He knows all of our dark secrets, and yet, He wants nothing more than to receive us as His own. Why? Because He loves us endlessly and wants us to find the freedom we are so desperately seeking—a freedom found only in Him. He calls to us to find rest in Him.

> For everyone has sinned; we all fall short of God's glorious standard. (*Rom. 3:23*, NLT)

Although we may feel as though our lives are meaningless or beyond repair, God knows what amazing things we're capable of if we only trust Him. He desires us to come to Him just as we are and to seek Him. How do we seek Him? Growing up I heard an acronym for the word *Bible* that was fitting: **B**asic **I**nstructions **B**efore **L**eaving **E**arth.

We discover Him by reading, by spending time with Him daily in prayer and worship, by attending a Bible- based church and hearing sound teaching. The more we seek Him, the more He reveals Himself to us. The more He reveals Himself to us, the more we grow. If we ask, He will forgive us of all the messed up things we've done. Satan wants us to believe that we are the only ones who have failed in certain areas. He wants us to believe we are beyond God's forgiveness and healing. I want you to know that you are not the first person to do whatever it is that you've done, and you won't be the last. God has forgiven millions before you, and He will forgive you and the millions who come after you.

> If we confess our sins, He is faithful and just to forgive
> us our sins and to cleanse us from all unrighteousness.
> (*1 John 1:9*, ESV)

> But God shows His love for us in that while we were
> still sinners, Christ died for us. (*Rom. 5:8*, ESV)

Satan uses the same tactics over and over again. He tells us that we are not worthy of God, that God is not real, that He is void of power, and that God won't forgive us for the horrible things we've done.

All lies.

Satan cannot tell the truth. John 8:44 says about Satan, "…When he lies, he speaks out of his own character, for he is a liar and the father of lies."

This is the reason it is so important to read the Bible. The Bible is truth—John 8:32 NIV says, "Then you will know the truth, and the truth will set you free." There is only one God, and He is the same yesterday, today, and forever (Heb. 13:8). Come to Christ just as you are and allow Him to work in you. If you don't allow God to be God in your life, your life will never change.

So many people say that God is number one in their lives, but is that really true? Do we give God as much attention as we give to our significant others? Do we think about Christ throughout the day, keeping Him at the center of everything we do? If He is the center of our lives, our lives should reflect Christ. Unfortunately, it took a few years after accepting Christ into my heart before my life started looking like a Proverbs 31 woman (a godly woman).

Spiritual Warfare

You can be free but not filled.

When we come to a place of brokenness, saying, "I can't do this anymore on my own; God save me," we are acknowledging our inability to save ourselves from the destruction around us, and instead, making the decision to accept the free gift offered to us through Jesus Christ: the gift that will set us free, the gift of salvation. Salvation is simply the act of accepting Jesus as our one and only Lord and Savior. Salvation restores the relationship between God and mankind that was severed when Adam and Eve sinned. Jesus lived a life free of sin, and after three years of ministry, He paid for the sins of mankind (including you and me) by dying on the cross and enduring the penalty we truly deserve, which is eternal death.

Why do we deserve death? In the Garden of Eden, everything was perfect, but because Adam and Eve disobeyed God, sin was ushered into the world. Since that time, every human being born has been born a sinner. Most will say, "That's not fair!" Romans 5:19 KJV says, "For as by one man's (Adam's) disobedience many were made sinners, so by the obedience of One [Jesus] shall many be made righteous." Jesus came to bridge the gap between God and man; we can't do it in our own strength. We are incapable of living a sinless life.

When Jesus was crucified on the cross, He died, went to hell, and paid the penalty and took the punishment for our sins. Jesus took the keys of hell and the grave and gives us the opportunity to have eternal life in heaven. He gave His life for our sins to cleanse us, make us new, and bring us into right relationship with God. When we sin, we can ask God to forgive us, and He will. He sets us back on our feet, dusts us off, and tells us to keep going.

During childhood, most are taught right from wrong and learn from their mistakes not to repeat previous actions that got them into bad situations. Following Christ is similar. As we develop a relationship with Christ through Bible reading, praying, worshiping, etc., we learn, grow, and mature. As we do so, we find ourselves rarely making the same mistakes over and over. Instead, we become strong in and through Jesus, and overcome those things that once would have been stumbling blocks for us.

> For God so loved the world, that he gave his only
> Son, that whoever believes in him should not perish

> but have eternal life. For God did not send his Son into the world to condemn the world, but in order that the world might be saved through him. (*John 3:16–17*, ESV)

> Because, if you confess with your mouth that Jesus is Lord and believe in your heart that God raised Him from the dead, you will be saved. For with the heart one believes and is justified, and with the mouth one confesses and is saved. (*Rom. 10:9–10*, ESV)

Without receiving Jesus Christ into our hearts and following His Word, the Bible, we are all destined to spend eternity in hell. Sounds harsh, I know, but it's true. No matter how we try to get around it or flat out ignore it, we are making a choice. We choose either Jesus or Satan. When we choose Jesus, Colossians 1:13 NLT says, "For he has rescued us from the kingdom of darkness and transferred us into the Kingdom of His dear Son." There are only two kingdoms: darkness (Satan's kingdom) or light (Jesus' kingdom).

Many think they have a third option such as atheism, their own set of beliefs, a false religion, etc. The problem with choosing neither Jesus nor Satan is that, by choosing neither, they *are* choosing Satan. I like this analogy: On one side of the fence is Jesus; on the other side of the fence is Satan. When someone says, "I choose the fence because I don't want to choose Jesus or Satan." Satan snatches them and says, "I own the fence."

After acknowledging Jesus as my Savior, my life looked nothing like I expected it to look. I was still drinking heavily, cursing, smoking, entertaining suicidal thoughts, clubbing occasionally, going to strip clubs, and succumbing to negative feelings about life or myself. Although I read the Bible and went to church every Sunday, during the week, intense battles with my flesh consumed me.

People can be forgiven in Jesus, having accepted salvation, while at the same time, not be filled with the Word of God. It is not uncommon to see people who profess to be Christians but whose lives look like anything but Christian. They are quick to throw out popular Scriptures such as Luke 6:37 (NLT): "Do not judge others, and you will not be judged."

Ask them about the context of the Scripture: who is speaking? Who is the audience? What prompted the speaker to address this group? Most of the time, they will have no answer to these questions. To really understand a verse, we need to understand the whole chapter. In order to understand the whole chapter, we need to understand that specific Book. In order to understand the Book, we need to know who is talking and to whom they are talking.

We can't watch two minutes of a movie and expect to understand it. That's silly. Likewise, we can't walk around claiming Christianity when we couldn't care less about studying, learning, and growing in it.

When people are not filled with the Word of God, Satan has a field day with them. Satan doesn't quit once you've received Jesus into your heart. If anything, he doubles his efforts because he doesn't want to lose you, and he changes his method of trying to reach you. He tries to get us to think that if we have a semblance of love for God in our hearts and know a few Scriptures, we're good. Right?

Wrong! So many fall victim to this trap. I hear all the time, "God is a loving God, and He knows my heart." Yes, He is a loving God. Yes, He knows your heart. He does not, however, say, "Okay, you can sin and not follow the Bible because you have a *type* of love for Me."

> And he answered, "You shall love the Lord your God with all your heart and with all your soul and with all your strength and with all your mind, and your neighbor as yourself." (Luke 10:27, ESV)

This verse puts God first and us second in everything we do. Is God the center of our lives? If He is, then our lives should look more and more like the life and personality of Jesus (1 John 2:6). And for those who have a form of love for God but not God's definition of love for Him, one day He will judge your heart...what will He find?

God hates sin and opposes the proud. What makes us think that we should get a free pass or that we can put the Bible on the shelf and never open it, assuming that "the way we see it" is fine by God's standards? If we take the time to read the Bible, we will see exactly what God does with people who think their thinking is as good as or above His knowledge. It is not pretty.

When we accept Jesus Christ as our Lord and Savior, God's new nature, His Spirit, comes to live inside of us. Our old nature was crucified on the cross with Jesus and is now replaced with God's nature. Satan has an immediate eviction notice. At that moment, he has to leave. Not one day later or two minutes later, but right then and there, immediately. Now that Satan is evicted, we have to fill the house (body, soul, and spirit) with Christ. Otherwise, Satan and his goons will come back, checking to see if the house is still empty, and if so, they will move right back in, bringing a few more demon buddies with them. Not fun.

> When an evil spirit comes out of a man, it goes through arid places seeking rest and does not find it. Then it says, "I will return to the house I left." When it arrives, it finds the house unoccupied, swept clean and put in order. Then it goes and takes with it seven other spirits more wicked than itself, and they go in and live there. And the final condition of that man is worse than the first. That is how it will be with this wicked generation. (Matt. 12:43–45, NIV)

What does this look like?

Lies, distraction, ignorance, and deception. Satan will do his best to distract us or fill our minds with wrong thinking in an attempt to continue to have control over our lives. Satan will try to distract us with the busyness of our daily lives, and we will believe his lies, that we don't have time to go to church, read the Bible, or pray. When this becomes a daily distraction, too easily we stray away from the faith and back into old habits.

Satan deceives some people by feeding them the lie that God accepts homosexuality. It's easier to justify a sin than it is to take the difficult road toward freedom. By twisting the Word of God, those who haven't gone directly to the source (Bible and God) for answers, accept false doctrines and theories, and many begin to immerse themselves in LGBTQ-affirming churches.

The question is asked, "What's wrong with LGBTQ-affirming churches?" When we affirm anything contrary to the Word of God, no matter what it is, we are basically walking right into the arms of Satan.

> So whoever knows the right thing to do and fails to do it, for him it is sin. (*James 4:17*, ESV)

> For the wages of sin is death, but the free gift of God is eternal life in Christ Jesus our Lord. (*Rom. 6:23*, ESV)

We cannot take the easy way out. Billions of people have found freedom from homosexuality, alcoholism, greed, pornography, etc. I think one of the biggest problems we face is that it's easier to find individuals who say change is not possible than it is to find people who say, "God delivered me." Those of us who have been delivered are many, and we are out there. Yes, it's hard; it may even be the most difficult thing you will ever walk out of, but God is powerful. He is faithful, and He will deliver those who set themselves to know God, those who choose to let Jesus live His life in and through them. Looking back, I wouldn't have changed a thing. If God did it for me, He can do it for you.

8 My Story: Tugging

Age: Twenty-seven

fter about two years of dating, Aaliyah, my little princess, and I were quite comfortable. They met my family and I met Aaliyah's. Her family was loving and kind and immediately made me feel welcome. My mother loved the two of them dearly and was always excited to see them. She treated my princess like her granddaughter. She delighted in buying things for them and enjoyed making my princess happy. My mother had come a long way from her homophobic rants to being super accepting and loving toward the homosexual community. Many times my mother would take Aaliyah's side when an argument ensued, and I would get scolded, but I didn't mind. I loved the fact that my mother loved the woman I loved.

My father, on the other hand, had learned to be nice to the women I dated, but he was anything but accepting of the relationships. I did, however, appreciate his kindness toward them in spite of his beliefs.

Close to the two-year mark in Aaliyah's and my relationship, I spoke with my parents about my wanting to marry her. I still can't believe how I mustered up the strength to do such a bold thing, but I did. Deep down, I desired the blessings of my mother and father to marry her. One day I called them and discussed my thoughts and feelings about Aaliyah's and my future.

Even though I knew what my father's response would be, I was still saddened when I heard it. He was quiet on the other end of the line while I spoke. Then he said, "You know how I feel about it, but if it makes you happy..."

From my mother, I had expected a different tune. As happy as she was with my relationship with Aaliyah and her daughter, she also went quiet. Because of her reservations, she paused before she responded, "If you are happy, that is all that matters."

I knew that not everyone I loved would feel comfortable about a wedding, but it's what you do when you love someone, and I loved Aaliyah with everything in me. But in the back of my mind, having a traditional wedding bothered me. Who would come? If my close family did come, would they be there with disappointment in their eyes and hearts, secretly talking behind our backs about how we were out of God's will?

As I began to seriously contemplate asking Aaliyah to marry me, something began stirring on the inside of me. I didn't recognize what it was at first. I just knew that I felt some type of hesitancy or discomfort. Assuming it was just the nervousness about making such a life-changing decision, I ignored it.

A month or two later, a Christian coworker and I were heading home together from work when that uneasy feeling began plaguing me. I took advantage of being alone with him in the car and asked his opinion about the feelings I was having. I told him that every time I started thinking about proposing or about marriage; I would sense uneasiness deep inside. My stomach would often churn at the thought of taking that next step with Aaliyah.

When I told my coworker that I didn't understand what was happening, his answer was simple and loving. He said, "That's conviction."

At that moment, I felt like an atomic bomb had dropped inside of me, inundating me with an intense sinking feeling in the pit of my stomach. I immediately understood it all. As he continued, I sat with tears rolling down my face, thinking, *This can't be happening. I don't want this to happen!*

He continued, "God is trying to tell you that living this kind of life is not what He wants for you. This is how God speaks to us—by a gentle tug." After that he was silent.

I said nothing as I tried to stop the tears gushing from my eyes. Immediately I thought about what I had told God right before I left for college: *That I was tired of the conviction, and for Him to spend time with Satan in Hades; that I wanted nothing to do with Him; that I wanted Him to leave me alone.* After choosing to reject God that day, I forgot what conviction felt like.

Sitting there in the car with my coworker, I was not ready for the reality that hit me. It terrified me, and I knew that I was not ready to open the door that would change my life. So I chose to ignore it.

Over the course of three months or so, these feelings often haunted me. Toward the end of July 2011, I was at home alone on my day off. My little princess was visiting her grandparents for the summer, and Aaliyah was at work. I began to feel the uneasiness and doubt rising up in me again. It seemed as though these feelings had gotten stronger over time, and that day they came to a head. I had what I wanted most, which was Aaliyah, my princess, a house, a dog, and a white picket fence.

But there was something still missing from my American dream—a void no human can fill. I knew that God was trying to get my attention, waiting patiently until I was ready. And He knew that I was, in fact, now ready. He was offering me a freedom He knew I desired (whether I knew it at the moment or not), but He also knew that I was scared of leaving the only lifestyle in which I felt comfortable.

I was tired of running from what God was trying to say to me. I realized that, yes, I had a "relationship" with God, but it was totally one-sided. I was living my life the way *I wanted.* I realized that although God was not at the fore front of my life, I knew I loved Him, and deep down inside me, I wanted more of Him, so it was time to stop running.

During the previous two years, I'd read the Bible, front to back, and I knew that Jesus had the power to heal, to save, to restore, and to deliver. Biblical stories about the worst of the worst coming to Jesus and finding complete peace began to invade my thoughts. I read stories of defiant people who experienced God's mercy and love and stories of what happened to people who chose to ignore Him and lived as gods of their own lives. I now understood that the god I had created for myself over the years was a god of destruction, deceit, confusion, and lies; the god I had created was *not* the God of the Bible.

Right then and there, I fell on my knees in my living room. No words came from my lips, but my uncontrollable tears and broken heart spoke volumes. I was submitting to the one true King, the Lord of lords, the Alpha and Omega, the only One Who has power to save! As I was crying out to God, a Bible passage that I had read a few days earlier popped into my mind—the story of Gideon and the fleece. In the book of Judges chapter 6, God gave Gideon an assignment. Gideon, riddled by doubt and knowing that there was no way in the natural to carry out God's order, asked God to confirm the assignment.

> Then Gideon said to God, "If You will save Israel by my hand, as You have said, behold, I am laying a fleece of wool on the threshing floor. If there is dew on the fleece alone, and it is dry on all the ground, then I shall know that You will save Israel by my hand, as You have said." And it was so. When he rose early next morning and squeezed the fleece, he wrung enough dew from the fleece to fill a bowl with water. Then Gideon said to God, "Let not Your anger burn against me; let me speak just once more. Please let me test just once more with the fleece. Please let it be dry on the fleece only, and on all the ground let there be dew." And God did so that night; and it was dry on the fleece only, and on all the ground there was dew. (Judg. 6:36–40, ESV)

I decided to take the same approach. I thought if God is such a big and mighty God, then He can answer me in the same manner. I cried out to God, "God, if You're telling me that it's wrong to be with women, that it's wrong to live a homosexual lifestyle, then fine, I'm ready to listen. But I need to know if it's *really You* talking to me, and that I am not just freaking out or having some sort of meltdown. If this is really You, please do three things for me so I have no doubt that it's You speaking to me: (1) Have Aaliyah bring up the topic of homosexuality and Christianity. If you do that, then I will tell her what you're telling me (that homosexuality is against God's Word, and we cannot do this anymore), and I will break up with her; (2) I need the breakup conversation to happen peacefully; and (3) please give me peace about it all."

Prior arguments between the two of us could easily end in screaming and yelling because neither of us wanted to budge. We both wanted to be consoled by the other, and if one of us did break and console the other, it was usually I who gave in to her.

Although I was doing my best to follow Christ, during tough times I still dealt with depression, cutting, and suicidal thoughts. I didn't want this breakup to get the best of me. I was scared that I wouldn't be able to cope with losing the woman I loved more than life itself. She was everything I wanted in a woman, and if I regretted my decision and lost her forever, I didn't know what I would do.

After I finished talking to God, I got up, dried my face, and went on with my day. That night when she got home from work, I acted normally and gave her no reason to suspect what happened earlier with me. The next day I got up and went to work as usual. I honestly was not even thinking about the day before, partially because I badly wanted for it to *not* have been God talking to me. I would have enjoyed believing that it was just my nerves because I was trying to make such a huge decision.

While at work, I got a call from Aaliyah. I can't remember why she called, but as we talked, something she said made my heart start racing, and I almost dropped the phone. She began talking about someone she knew, and how deep down, she didn't know of a single homosexual who felt 100 percent comfortable about being *homosexual and Christian* because of their deep-seated convictions.

I don't recall ever having such a conversation with her, and this was certainly out of the norm for her to bring up such a topic. I knew that I had to make the next move. I proceeded to tell her that God had been convicting me about the very same topic, and that I had to follow what God was telling me. I couldn't run from it anymore. I told her I loved her so much, but I wanted to love God more.

I was thunderstruck when she said, "Jessica, I will never go against what God is telling someone." I was blown away by her response. If there was a time to yell, cry, and argue, this was the time. But it didn't happen.

God had just done two of the three things I had asked. I was stunned. My mind was racing. I couldn't believe what was happening, and my emotions were all over the place. When I hung up the phone, I stood there in shock. My coworker asked if I was all right. I just smiled and said, "You have no idea how okay I am."

When my shift was almost over, I received another call from Aaliyah. This time she was anything but calm. After soaking in the gravity of our conversation, she began having second thoughts. As I listened to her, sensing her raw emotions, I felt nothing but the peace of God. *Peace* was my third request of God. Perfect peace washed through me. I had no sadness, depression, or confusion. I had never felt like this during a breakup with any ex.

In twenty-four hours, God had given me exactly what I had asked for. He had answered positively all three requests, and at that moment, I knew something had changed. I knew I would never be the same again. I was all in for Jesus.

> Then you will experience God's peace, which exceeds
> anything we can understand. His peace will guard
> your hearts and minds as you live in Christ Jesus.
> (Phil. 4:7, NLT)

The month it took for Aaliyah to move out of our house was extremely tough. I continued to have peace about the breakup and especially about leaving homosexuality, but she was distraught. Since Princess was with the grandparents for the summer, Aaliyah moved out of our bedroom and started sleeping in Princess's room. Every night I could hear her cry herself to sleep and then cry in her sleep, and my heart broke for her. I never wanted to hurt her. She was hurting so badly I would have given anything to make her hurt go away, but the only thing that would make it better, she couldn't have. I hated seeing her cry. If I had not had God's peace, I wouldn't have made it.

It got so bad that I had her sleep on the couch while I slept on the floor next to her holding her hand and trying to comfort her so she could fall asleep in peace. She would fall asleep but continue to cry while sleeping. Seeing Aaliyah hurting was excruciating for me. When the couch sleeping arrangement didn't help, I had her sleep in the bed with me. As I wrapped my arms around her and held her tightly, I felt slightly uncomfortable.

Lying in bed together, we talked. Despite my not wanting to, but out of misplaced compassion for her, we had sex. For the first time *ever* in my life, I felt repulsed by the act. Although I was used to having sex with women and enjoyed every aspect of it thoroughly, I saw what I was doing at that moment with new eyes. I thought to myself, *This is disgusting!* I wanted it to be over as soon as possible. I felt like I had violated myself, which I had.

In all of the one-night stands with women I hardly knew, I never felt uncomfortable after sex. But after God answered my three-part *fleece*, and I fully surrendered my life to God, I was a new person. "Therefore if any man be in Christ, he is a **new** creature: old things are passed away; behold, all things are become **new**" (2 Cor. 5:17; emphasis mine). I don't remember feeling that I had just sinned with Aaliyah, but I did feel bad. A few months after this incident, the light bulb flashed on in my head that yes, I had sinned with her, and I quickly repented.

When Aaliyah moved out of the house, I was relieved yet saddened that she was gone. Our future, our plans had all vanished. Don't get me wrong, I had and still have peace that my choice was right. But even while resting in the peace of God, I began to miss her. I began to miss the love we shared, the good times we had, and memories we created.

I was starting a new chapter in my life, and I knew everything would be different. I was scared, excited, and worried about how it would be. I had a million questions for God, but I had no answers. I felt like I was given a parachute and told to jump out of a plane, but I had no clue as to how to make the parachute open.

Tugging

> But now I am going to him who sent me, and none of you asks me, "Where are you going?" But because I have said these things to you, sorrow has filled your heart. Nevertheless, I tell you the truth: it is to your advantage that I go away, for if I do not go away, the Helper [the Holy Spirit] will not come to you. But if I go, I will send him to you. And when he comes, he will convict the world concerning sin and righteousness and judgment...When the Spirit of truth comes, he will guide you into all the truth, for he will not speak on his own authority, but whatever he hears he will speak, and he will declare to you the things that are to come. (John 16:5–8, 13)

The Holy Spirit is given to each born-again believer the moment we accept Jesus Christ as our Lord and Savior. We need the Holy Spirit for many reasons, and I've listed a few:

To live in us

While Jesus lived on this earth for only thirty-three years, He had a major impact upon the world. He cured the incurable, saved those who were destined for an eternity in hell, and ministered the Word of God to a lost and dying world. Jesus died on the cross, rose on the third day, and before He left to be with His Father in heaven, He told His disciples that He would send us a helper. That helper is the Holy Spirit. Through the Holy Spirit, we as believers in Jesus Christ are equipped to do what Jesus has already commanded us to do. What has God commanded believers to do? We are called to fulfill the *Great Commission*:

Now the eleven disciples went to Galilee, to the mountain to which Jesus had directed them. And when they saw Him they worshiped Him, but some doubted. And Jesus came and said to them, "All authority in heaven and on earth has been given to Me. Go therefore and **make disciples** of all nations, **baptizing them** in the name of the Father and of the Son and of the Holy Spirit, **teaching them** to observe all that I have commanded you. And behold, I am with you always, to the end of the age." (Matt. 28:16–20, ESV; emphasis mine)

Afterward He [Jesus] appeared to the eleven themselves as they were reclining at table, and He rebuked them for their unbelief and hardness of heart, because they had not believed those who saw Him after He had risen. And He said to them, "Go into all the world and proclaim the gospel to the whole creation. Whoever believes and is baptized will be saved, but whoever does not believe will be condemned. And these signs will accompany those who believe: in My Name they will cast out demons; they will speak in new tongues; they will pick up serpents with their hands; and if they drink any deadly poison, it will not hurt them; they will lay their hands on the sick, and they will recover."

So then the Lord Jesus, after He had spoken to them, was taken up into heaven and sat down at the right hand of God. And they went out and preached everywhere, while the Lord worked with them and confirmed the message by accompanying signs. (Mark 16:14–20, ESV)

By the Holy Spirit living within us, we are able to carry out all the work that God has called for us to do here on earth. Many feel that they can't carry out some of these mandates, but that is not true. Growing up in an environment where casting out demons, laying on of hands, and healing the sick was not talked about, I felt that those gifts were only for certain individuals who were extra spiritual. NOT TRUE! In a nutshell, we all have a measure of faith. There is nothing different between powerful ministers such as Billy Graham and Oral Roberts and you. They just took the time to walk with God and develop their relationships with our Creator. You see, the more we exercise our faith, the stronger it becomes. Just like working out, we cannot expect to be lean and fit overnight. We have to take the time to work out daily, then, over time, we become stronger. Our faith in Jesus and what He has called us to do is similar. Daily we have to develop our relationship with Jesus, our understanding of the Bible, and our gaining knowledge and wisdom. Over time we become stronger in our faith and in who we are meant to be in Christ. Through our life in Him, we begin to understand that we can do the things Jesus commanded us to do.

To convict us of what is right and wrong

The Holy Spirit convicts us of what is right and wrong, tugs on us when we need to change directions or when we need to minister to someone. The Holy Spirit warns us when we are about to do the wrong thing, etc. The tugs of the Holy Spirit are endless.

Also, when God is dealing with an unbeliever, He will tug on them as well. God tugs on unbelievers so that He can make Himself known to them. God desires each person to be saved and free from Satan's grasp. If we look back on our lives, we might realize there were several times when God was tugging at our hearts. Many times an unbeliever may not know that these tugs are coming from God.

For example, during my adolescent and college years, I felt like it was Satan who was trying to trip me up when I had doubts about living a homosexual lifestyle or being a homosexual Christian. I went with what I felt was right in my heart, wanting my life to be acceptable to God. I know now that the tugging was not from Satan trying to make me miserable, but rather from God, Who was trying to tell me that my life was going in the wrong direction. Another example: People would, with compassion for me, tell me that I drank too much, and I'd immediately get defensive. I got defensive because deep down, I knew that they might be right. I now see this was not an attack against me, but it was God speaking through them to help me. My own defensiveness would rise up, harden my heart, and cause me to quickly reject what they were saying.

When conflict was warring inside me over the issue of homosexuality, I now realize it was God tugging on me. God was tugging on me when I'd cry at night, hating myself for not being able to change. God was tugging on me when I wrote that twenty-five-page term paper, *Homosexuality and the Bible*. God was tugging on me when I was cutting. God was tugging on me every time I stepped into a church or when I was in close proximity to Bible-believing Christians. God was tugging on me when people spoke to me about Jesus, and I chose to ignore them because the possibility of their being right terrified me. God was tugging on me as I tried to drown my problems in alcohol. God was tugging on me every time I was arrested. God was tugging on me when I was being raped. God was tugging on me when I started buying clothes from the men's section. And God was tugging on me when I wanted to spend the rest of my life with the woman I loved so deeply.

God will continue to tug on our hearts to get our attention. We think we know what is best for our lives, but only God knows the plans He has for us (Jer. 29:11). He knows that the one person we desperately need in our lives is Jesus. He will continue to tug and encourage us to accept Jesus into our hearts before we take our last breath.

To guide us along the journey which is life

The Holy Spirit is the guide who helps us understand and interpret the Word of God. The Bible tells us that the old us is gone, and we are now new creations in Christ Jesus. Now that we are new creations, our lives will change drastically if we allow God to work in us and through us. Although we are the same person, Jesus becomes the center of our lives, and we become kingdom minded. Christ and His desires, His plans, and His work become our focus. Many people think they will somehow become mindless, brainwashed Jesus freaks and be totally boring individuals once they give their lives to Jesus. I used to say that, thinking that there would be no fun in being one of *those Christians*. But that is not true. When we immerse ourselves in God and His Word, life takes on whole new dimensions. Receiving Jesus as the Savior of our lives is the most exciting thing anybody can ever do!

God has a calling for each of us, and it's not simply to charge blindly through life without direction or purpose. God doesn't want us to live to work and work to live. He has a plan, and the Holy Spirit is there to guide us in His divine purpose for each of us. Some may be called to pastor or evangelize; all are called to witness in their local communities, on the job, or in their families. God wants to reach every human being in this world, and He wants to use us to do it.

As we seek God and develop a relationship with Him, He will faithfully guide us. No matter what we think about ourselves (too young, too smart, or too stupid), with God's help we can fulfill the calling He has ordained for our lives. Whatever He calls us to do, He is faithful to equip us with the things we need to carry out His plan.

9 My Story: Freedom

Age: Twenty-seven to Present

After Aaliyah moved out, I began to feel the emptiness of her not being a part of my life. I often thought, *What on earth did I just do? The most important person in my life was gone. My future plans and everything that made me happy before vanished.* Not knowing what to do, I began to let my emotions get the best of me. On several occasions I cried myself to sleep because of the hurt of losing her, as well as the drastic life change, had become overwhelming. Night after night, I allowed Satan to comfort me with negativity and confusion. After a while, I became sick of being in a place of misery, so I decided to call Robert, my college friend and old party buddy. We had met during my freshman year of undergrad, and we quickly became friends. Because Robert was a few years older, he usually supplied the alcohol for our get-togethers. When I was a sophomore, he got me a weekend job at a T.G.I. Friday's back home. Most weekends we drove the two and a half hours back home with other friends, and, with the exception of the driver, enjoyed drinking alcohol along the way. After graduation, friends went their separate ways, and Robert seemed to disappear off the grid.

When I got saved in 2008, I learned that Robert began following Christ after a series of setbacks of his own. I was happy to hear that someone from my past was now on the same journey as me. We could encourage and uplift one another as well as relate to each other's past hurts and old lifestyles. With Robert, I could be totally transparent. It was a blessing to know that not all old friendships were gone after I chose to follow Christ.

Not knowing that my newfound revelation would repel some of my closest friends who were homosexual, I told them what God had done in my life. I wanted to share God's love and truth with the world. I just knew that if I told them, they would begin to see clearly and be set free from the bondage they never knew they were in.

Was I ever wrong! They couldn't understand why I flipped the script on them. They thought I had gone nuts. It was then that I began to experience a drift from many of my LGBTQ affirming friendships. I thought that these friendships would remain the same although we had different opinions, but I was in for a rude awakening.

The LGBTQ community that I once stood with for equality, tolerance, same-sex marriages, and stood with them in calling Christians and others alike on their hypocrisy and hate toward us turned on me and began spewing the same hatred and intolerance for my newfound beliefs. Oh, the irony.

The Bible, God's Word, does a good job at explaining these behaviors. "A fool takes no pleasure in understanding, but only in expressing his opinion" (Prov. 18:2 ESV). I remember all of the years I claimed to say I understood others' opinions, but deep down, I didn't really open my mind and heart...I couldn't have them be right, especially concerning a lifestyle to which I was committed.

I called Robert that day. I told him that God had opened my eyes to a whole new world that I had once swore didn't exist, but as excited as I was, I was also scared of the unknown. He reassured me that everything was going to be all right.

He also told me that after Aaliyah and I had gone to visit his wife and him a couple of months earlier, his wife told him that God had assured her that He (God) was about to move in our lives. Robert admitted thinking that was pretty farfetched and unlikely to happen. But here I was, having done a 180-degree turn in my thinking. Robert was blown away and excited.

He told me that I should check out a twelve-step program

called Celebrate Recovery (CR) that could help me transition out of homosexuality. He told me that CR is a nationwide, twelve-step, Christ-centered recovery program that would support me in all I was going through. The problem was not only that I needed assistance in my transition from homosexuality, but I had an array of deep-seated issues that God needed to work on. After Robert finished explaining the program, I wasn't interested in going at all. I didn't want to sit in a circle with a group of strangers and talk about my problems. How was that going to solve anything?

As weeks went on, I was beginning to feel discouraged. I had no one to turn to or talk to who understood what Christ had done in my life. It seemed as though every homosexual friend I had deserted me. They may not have come out and said it, but the silent segregation, due to the differences in beliefs between us, was clear. The main ingredient to our friendship no longer existed. Aside from that blow, it was difficult finding anyone to assist me from a Biblical base. It's one thing for a straight person with no experience to give advice on the topic of homosexuality, but it's a totally different thing when someone who has come out of that lifestyle can attest to God's delivering power.

Although I had peace about walking out of the homosexual lifestyle, depression, fear, and discouragement continued to haunt me. I no longer wanted to live in the house that held so many memories of the woman with whom I was once ready to spend the rest of my life. Everything in the house made me think of her, my little princess, and the love we shared. On top of it all, I hated my job, and I hated South Texas. It was unbearable.

In spite of these feelings, I was still excited about what God had done in my life, and I was not about to turn back now. Because He had already done "the impossible" in my life, I was curious as to how much better it could get if I give Him my all.

I asked Him to show me how big a God He really is through my own personal journey here on earth, and I asked Him to use me for His glory. I made a commitment; I was all in. I knew that things weren't going to be easy, but I knew that it was going to be worth it. I began talking about Jesus to everyone around me.

With that being said, I quickly became a human repellant for many people—current friends and old. Whether people wanted to hear it or not, I'd give them an overdose of God. It seemed the harder I tried, the worse I made things. A few months later, I learned that pushing Jesus on people was not the way to share Christ, but, in fact, it was the perfect way to push people away from Him.

Eventually I accepted Robert's advice to attend CR. He told me that the only one in the area was at a church called The Family Church (TFC), quite close to where I lived, and the meetings were held on Friday nights. When he said this, I recalled that during the previous weeks, several people at my workplace mentioned this church and told me to check it out, but I had always shrugged off the invitations. I had my small Baptist church that I attended and was comfortable there. When Robert said that this was the only church in the whole area that had this program, I felt like God was trying to tell me to also check out the church services there, but I was not ready to try something new just yet.

At the beginning of October 2011, I attended Celebrate Recovery at The Family Church for the first time, and I hated it. It wasn't just the program but the whole church environment, which was so different from what I was used to. I was used to gospel music that was rooted in the African-American culture as well as its history. What was this Hillsong, Jesus Culture, and Bethel Worship music? As everyone stood and worshipped, I slouched in the chair in my sweatshirt and baggy sweatpants, arms crossed and legs parted in defiance.

For the first few weeks of attending the program, I physically would be present, but I was not always mentally there. I told Robert that I wasn't going back because I couldn't stand it. With a bit of urging on his part, I promised Robert that I would give it a month, and that was all. Period. My mind often drifted somewhere else while I sat on that cold folding chair. Sometimes my thoughts drifted to Aaliyah, or to doubts such as, *Is this really going to all work out? Will I ever like guys the way I love girls?* I often thought, *If God did something so amazing in my life, then why do I feel so horrible now?*

Having no real desire to get up and attend the meetings, I'd throw on black sweatpants and a baggy T-shirt and drive to CR. Sweatpants and sweatshirts were my security blankets. I felt I could hide my feelings behind the loose- fitting clothes, sort of like a child dragging a nasty little blanket along the floor, refusing to have it washed.

During one of the CR meetings, we were told about the twenty-five-week long, in-depth step study that is offered in small group settings. The study is designed to dig deeper into our hurts, habits, and hang-ups, allowing God to work on the nitty-gritty aspects of our lives. I knew this would be a good thing since I had unanswered questions, and I knew I couldn't move forward until I had answers.

I needed to know how I got to this place. If I wasn't born a homosexual, how did I become one? Until I knew these answers, I felt stuck.

Near the end of October, I began the small group step study that CR offered. Through the step study, God began to reveal to me not only how I got caught up in the homosexual lifestyle, but He also opened my eyes and heart to the lies and deceits that had bound me to wrong thinking. I was blown away.

I began to see Satan's involvement throughout my whole life, but overshadowing it was God's hand and love beckoning me. Uncontrollable tears streamed from my eyes as God revealed to me what the devil had blinded me to throughout my whole life. Tears fell like rain against my cheeks as I realized I had blamed God for the devil's actions in my life. I had cursed the One Who loved me unconditionally as I ignorantly chose to worship myself and Satan. My throat tightened as God reassured me that He never stopped loving me through it all, and He rejoiced because I was now home where I belonged. The fortress that I had built around myself because of my stubbornness and all my hurts was being invaded by the love of Jesus. He permeated my entire being, and I didn't know how to handle it. I felt as though I was not worthy of being called His daughter.

I realized that it was not my being perfect that He wanted, because I will never achieve perfection, but rather He was asking that I be willing to let Him love me. Letting Him love us is always the first step. I was humbled before Him. I stood in awe of a love I never thought existed, a grace that was unfailing, and forgiveness that had no strings attached.

He began the process of melting away the confusion, depression, fear, and discouragement that was encapsulating me. But this process takes time. We will battle familiar feelings as we continue to allow God to transform our hearts and minds from the old us, into the new, always reaching deep into God's Word for truth, power, and strength to continue our upward journey.

Over the next few months, I struggled with trying to quit smoking and drinking. I realized that I had become dependent upon these things to have fun and to relax. In college, it was easy to explain away the excessive drinking and smoking. Night after night of getting trashed, waking up to a massive hangover that didn't go away until 6:00 p.m. that evening, was the norm.

As I got older and began working, I noticed that I was unable to have fun without getting wasted. My eyes were opened to the gravity of this problem one afternoon when Aaliyah's daughter, my Princess, tried to make me feel better after a long day at work. When I came home from an extremely frustrating day, I sat down on the couch to unwind, and my little Princess brought me a beer. She was about nine or ten at the time and had gone to the refrigerator, grabbed one of my Coronas, opened the bottle with a bottle opener, and brought it to me. I couldn't believe that she knew how to open the bottle.

I will never forget what she said to me as she set the ice-cold Corona on the wooden TV tray in front of me. She smiled and said, "I know this will make you feel better, and when you're almost done, I'll get you another." Feeling she had done something special, she walked back into the kitchen.

I was crushed. What kind of example was I setting for her? I thought about this for a whole minute before I guzzled down the cold beer and waited for the next.

I thought it would be easier to quit drinking than to quit smoking cigarettes, but I was totally wrong. I attended a few parties and get-togethers held by coworkers during the end of that year and found it extremely difficult to be around alcohol and not drink. I couldn't have fun without it. Without my liquid courage, I was quiet and anti-social, and it was extremely uncomfortable. I often thought, *Am I* going to be boring for the rest of my life?

Right before the New Year of 2012, I again felt the tug to check out the Sunday services at The Family Church. Over the past month, I had to admit to myself that I was no longer being fed spiritually at the small Baptist church I was attending, so I decided to go ahead and check out the church where I had been attending CR.

It was New Year's Eve, and I was determined *not* to like TFC's church services. I pulled into the large parking lot, joined others scrambling for parking spots, and managed to find one near the front door. As I went to open the church door, one of the greeters welcomed me with open arms and a hug. She asked if this was my first time there.

Caught off guard by her friendliness, I uncomfortably replied, "Yes it is."

"Well, I am glad you're here and hope you like it, *Mija*," she said. *Mija* is a term of endearment in the Hispanic culture, a contraction of *Mi Hija*, meaning "my daughter." I was shocked that she used such a word for someone she didn't know. The friendliness and pleasantness of everyone overwhelmed me. I could see their love for God by how they loved others. They didn't judge others by outer appearances or skin color; they just loved.

Seeing this kind of love quickly began to shed light into the dark areas within me. My lack of trust for others, the discomfort in being loved, and my hardened shell quickly rose to the surface, illuminating areas of weakness. I was invaded by love from people who didn't know me.

Later in my walk with God, I realized I was always slightly uncomfortable with others showing me love because of the hurts and disappointments I had experienced throughout my childhood, adolescence, and adult years. I had built a huge barrier to keep myself from being hurt, which in turn blinded me to my own unresolved issues.

The Family Church congregation was large, not African-American, and they definitely didn't sing from hymnals or sing the traditional songs I was used to. I sat in the last row and compared the service to services in Baptist churches I had previously attended. I was not a fan of the service, but when Senior Pastor John Brady gave the morning message, it resounded deep within my heart.

Again I felt God invading my heart and speaking directly to me. Needless to say, every sermon thereafter had the same effect. Every Sunday he seems to speak directly to my specific circumstances. It was nice to become a part of a church that is led by the Holy Spirit. When the Holy Spirit leads pastors, God works wonders in the hearts of the congregants.

Pastor John Brady was engaging and relatable, something I hadn't seen in a very long time. Tears streamed down my face as I soaked in every word of the sermon. Pastor John spoke about how we need not isolate ourselves from the world simply because we are afraid to get dirty by interacting with unbelievers. He mentioned how we cannot remain stagnant in our Christian lives, but we must always be learning, growing, sharing, and serving.

This was exactly how I'd been feeling over the past few months. It was easier to isolate myself than deal with people who couldn't understand the changes I was undergoing. My mother was upset because I had broken up with Aaliyah. My friends thought I had lost my mind, and my father couldn't relate, at any level, to God's supernatural power. My whole world was changing, and I didn't know how to deal with it.

That Sunday, I switched churches. I never went back to the church I was attending and began attending TFC fulltime. I had asked God about this decision, and He reminded me, "You are supposed to go where you get fed." Surprisingly, over time, I fell in love with the music I once hated. God began to soften my heart, and I quickly began to love everything about this church. I can't imagine worshiping God without my newly found favorite worship bands like Hillsong, Bethel Worship, or Jesus Culture.

Soon after joining TFC, I signed up for the Grow and Transformation classes they offered during the week. The first class I took was entitled "Seeking Him." As I went inside the building for the first class, I felt a bit anxious. Fear of stepping into uncharted waters made me apprehensive and nervous. I was shy, quiet, and uncomfortable as I walked down the hall toward the classroom in my trusty sweatpants and hoodie.

Barely one step inside the classroom, fear gripped me, and I was about to turn to leave when a woman sitting at one of the large round tables smiled and waved for me to come inside. I hadn't met her before and was wondering if she thought I was someone else. Not wanting to be rude, I walked inside and sat at her table. With a welcoming smile on her face, she introduced herself as Mary, and asked my name. She simply wanted to love on me. Although I appeared uncomfortable on the outside, on the inside, the warmth of love felt quite good and much appreciated.

After a few minutes of conversation, the class began. "Seeking Him" was about transformation of the heart, understanding God's love, forgiveness, and grace, as well as extending these to others in our lives. I was understanding and hearing the Word of God in a fresh new way. Silently I cried as the teacher explained the foundation of Christianity and what Jesus is all about. God's love continued to invade my broken heart, and it was overwhelming. Every class I take at TFC, every sermon I hear, continues to propel me forward as I grow in my faith. God is orchestrating something beautiful.

As much as I hated South Texas, God told me to "pitch my tent," and I realized I was going to be stuck here for a while. Pitching my tent was something I was going to choose to ignore for a while. Constantly complaining and grumbling about how I hated South Texas, I often voiced my desire to move back home to the Maryland area. This thinking consumed my time and thoughts. Somehow, I thought that if I ignored what God said, He would change His mind. Wrong!

Over a span of five years, I applied for more than four hundred jobs throughout the United States. It was mentally draining for me to always be focusing on potential job opportunities that I never got. I was not willing to get comfortable where I was.

The area of South Texas known as the Rio Grande Valley is spread out along the southern tip of Texas. The Rio Grande River is all that separates the Valley from Mexico. I live just thirty minutes from the River. Approximately 91 percent of the people residing in the Valley are of Hispanic descent and are not particularly accustomed to African Americans.

To say the least, as an African-American, I didn't fit in. People often asked if they could touch my hair, or they asked questions pertaining to the African-American culture, which usually started with, "Is it true that black people…"

I think you get the picture that there are very few of "us" in the Valley.

I definitely considered the Valley to be my personal wilderness. Just like Moses led the Israelites through the wilderness for forty years, I was out of my comfort zone and thrown into what I used to call "the twilight zone." I knew God had placed me here to work on me, and He was going to do just that. But to pitch my tent here was not acceptable.

Nonetheless, God continued to clean me up from the inside out. In one of my first lessons here in the Valley, He showed me that I was no better than the environment I detested. He held up a mirror before my face, and I didn't like what I saw. I believe that we all have prejudicial thoughts or feelings somehow ingrained in us due to our upbringing or culture. But to recognize these thoughts and allow God to change the way we think is what matters.

One Saturday morning I attended a prayer meeting at TFC, and when I walked in, I noticed that everyone was speaking in tongues. I thought to myself, *Oh no! It's that Pentecostal church all over again.* I was apprehensive because I didn't understand. I questioned the authenticity of speaking in tongues, and frankly, it scared me.

I joined the group and timidly began praying in English. A little while later, a woman came up to me and began prophesying over me. At that time, I didn't quite understand all the gifts of the Holy Spirit, but I did know that God gave people different gifts to use during certain times. This woman knew nothing about me or about my past. She took my hands in hers, began speaking in tongues, and then interpreted what she was hearing from God. She said, "I (God) have broken your chains, now I am calling you to do My work—to minister to those who are going through what you went through." She said a few more things to me, but I don't feel at liberty to share them now. I was shocked and blown away by her prophecy.

I was grateful for what God had already done in my life, and to get married and have kids were the only other things on my agenda as far as *my* life plans were concerned. What the woman said was like a seed being planted deep in my spirit. It was the beginning of a long series of destiny steps. Over the next few months, I had dreams that would stir within me the plans and purpose that God was placing inside of me. I had several dreams where I was an evangelist. I would see myself in front of thousands, preaching to them about God's delivering power. Thinking they were over the top and not within my capability or reach, I kept these dreams and feelings to myself. I felt as though I was not smart enough. I had stage fright. I was an introvert, and I was uncomfortable around large groups of people. Large to me meant any group of more than ten.

As I watched my favorite TV pastors throughout the day, I began imitating the preaching styles of people like Bishop Jakes and especially Sheryl Brady. There is something about her that resonates with my spirit. While going about my daily activities at work, I'd envision myself speaking in front of large crowds. Sometimes I'd awaken in the middle of the night, preaching in my sleep, every time with an unquenchable fire in my belly. Sometimes I couldn't go back to sleep because I was so pumped up. It was like lighting a fuse to dynamite. Not knowing what to do with the fire, I would praise God in advance for what He was about to do. During that spring, I made an appointment to speak with my new pastor. To this day, I still don't know why I did that. I really didn't have anything to talk about, but the overwhelming need to share my testimony was burning within my heart, and I wanted to share it with the world. I proceeded to tell Pastor John about all that God had done in my life up to that point, and he was blown away.

First and foremost, he wanted me to continue to grow in the Word of God and in Christ. He told me to continue to develop my relationship with God, to read the New Testament, and to get back with him at the end of the summer. At that time he might be able to use me in ministry. He said it might be a good idea to volunteer with the youth on Wednesdays. I was thinking to myself, *What is he talking* about? I don't want to be used in ministry. I just wanted to tell *him that it's possible to be delivered from homosexuality in spite of what the world thinks. But to be used in ministry?*

Totally shocked, but playing off it, I said okay and left. I enjoyed preaching to an empty house, but to people? And for real? I don't think so. Before meeting with Pastor John, I had spent quite a bit of time trying to convince myself that the unquenchable fire God placed in me was not real because of all the disappointments I'd had throughout my life.

That summer, I began talking to and encouraging individuals at church who struggled with homosexuality. I started to enjoy helping others who wanted help with their struggles. I loved showing them that there is freedom through Jesus Christ. The Bible tells us:

> You are the light of the world. A city set on a hill cannot be hidden. Nor do people light a lamp and put it under a basket, but on a stand, and it gives light to all in the house. In the same way, let your light shine before others, so that they may see your good works and give glory to your Father Who is in heaven. (Matt. 5:14–16, ESV)

I had spent many years in total darkness, choosing to follow the ways of the world. When God opened my eyes to the truth, I couldn't contain it. Who wouldn't want to share with the world something of this magnitude? To know that everyone could have the same freedom as I had, and all I had to do was share this good news with people, while letting God do the rest, was amazing.

One day as I was watching a sermon by Joel Osteen; he was talking about praying bigger prayers. It pushed me to take all of what I was sensing deep down inside me and to be bold in asking God out loud for the impossible. That night I proceeded to do just that. I prayed and asked God

- for a God-fearing, faithful, loving husband;
- to become an evangelist and bring thousands to Christ; and
- for my family members to genuinely develop a relationship with Christ.

The next day as I was getting ready for work, I turned the TV to the Daystar network to watch Joni Lamb's *Table Talk* and to watch Bishop T.D. Jakes. As I was listening to the table talk discussion, I noticed that the women participating in the discussion were talking about the first time they preached the Word of God. They discussed the moments or events leading up to their being called to preach.

The discussion nurtured the seed that was planted in me a few weeks earlier by Pastor John. My spirit resonated with the subtle tugs from God while the women were talking. As I spent my mornings with Joni and the bishop, many of their sermons and teachings continued to stir the desire to preach the Gospel.

One weekend I went to a party at a coworker's house and was offered alcohol. For the first time in my life, I had no desire for it! I couldn't believe that I said no so effortlessly. On the inside, I praised God for that victory.

Later, I came to understand that Satan always tries to tempt us to return to the things from which we have been delivered, so we must always be vigilant.

Around February, I started having explicit sexual dreams. I dreamed that I was having sex with individuals from my past, as well as people I would never ever think of in such a manner. At first I thought that I was simply craving something that for so many years I'd had consistently, so I shrugged it off. I thought it was normal.

Over time the dreams became more and more realistic. On several occasions I'd fall asleep, and while in a dream state, it felt like something was on top of me having sex with me. I didn't understand it and had never before experienced anything like that. I knew there was no involvement on my part, and although I was asleep, I was conscious of what was going on. I was aware of everything that happened, every touch and every pleasurable moment.

It was like being blindfolded and handcuffed. I knew *what* was happening, but I couldn't *see* it happening with my natural eyes, but I could *feel* it happening. In order to break the sexual activity, I had to resist the temptation to continue this activity. I was not only freaked out, but I was also embarrassed by at how real it all felt as it continued several times a week. It had gotten so frequent and overwhelming that I had to speak to someone about it.

I called my friend Robert's wife, Jean, to discuss what was happening. Robert had told me earlier that Jean was experienced in spiritual warfare, and she would be the perfect person to talk to about these things. I explained to Jean all that was going on. After I finished, I waited in silence for her response, hoping that she could help me.

Jean explained to me what spiritual warfare was and the different things she had personally experienced in her life. As she seemingly made every demonic horror movie come to life, I freaked out. She was so calm and confident when she spoke of our authority as Christians over all the powers of darkness and how Christ working through us can make demons tremble and flee. I sat holding the phone with eyes and mouth wide open, wishing I had called her during daylight hours.

She informed me that demons can have sexual encounters with humans. Years earlier, if I had heard this, I would have thought the woman was crazy. But I knew that what I was experiencing now was neither natural nor normal. I asked her how to get rid of the demons. She said that as a believer, I needed to pray over my house, anoint it with oil, and command in Jesus' name that the demons leave.

The moment I got off the phone with her, I did just that. I immediately walked to my bathroom and got out a small bottle of anointing oil that someone had given me awhile back. I wasted no time praying over my house. I walked from room to room anointing each door and window. I anointed my bedposts and prayed over my bed. I wanted to give no demon entry into my house. I put the anointing oil on my forehead and prayed, rebuking all unclean spirits, and commanding in the name of Jesus that they stop harassing me and that they leave my dwelling place. I didn't feel anything spectacular happen, nor did I hear an audible sound from heaven.

No demon screamed as it left my house. I just believed that as a child of God, I had the authority through Jesus to command such things to leave. After that night, I never had an encounter like that again, but it was definitely not the last of my encounters with the spirit realm.

Soon individuals gravitated to me after they encountered the dark side of the spirit realm, such as seeing dark shadows or demons walk through their houses or hearing questionable sounds and footsteps when they were home alone. I personally have experienced these dark shadows roaming during the night, but I have come to understand that I do not have to fear them because in Christ I have complete authority over them. I also know that through these encounters, we as Christians are able to learn and grow in our faith. We then will be able to assist other believers, as well as nonbelievers, who have been overpowered or tormented by demon manifestations.

One Friday night in March, as Celebrate Recovery was ending, one of the leaders pulled me aside to chat. She gave me a Word from God that confirmed one of my secret prayers—a prayer I had verbalized only to God. It is amazing how God uses people to let us know that He hears us and will give us our hearts desires *if they align with His purposes* for our lives. And it's amazing how He puts His perfect purposes in our hearts so that we want what He wants. The woman caught me off guard when she asked if I spoke in tongues. I stood there like a deer caught in headlights. She asked, "Was that something you had been asking God for?"

I had never told *anyone* that I desired to speak in tongues because I didn't quite understand how it worked, and if it was just a bunch of people creating gibberish in their own might, I didn't want any part of it. Fortunately, we had just gone over a lesson about the Holy Spirit and the gift of tongues in one of my small-group classes at church. I learned what speaking in tongues was all about. I learned that there is a prayer language as well as the gift of tongues, which operates alongside the gift of interpretation.

Gift of Tongues to edify the church:

If any speak in a tongue, let there be only two or at most three, and each in turn, and let someone interpret. But if there is no one to interpret, let each of them keep silent in church and speak to himself and to God. (1 Cor. 14:27–28, ESV)

Tongues, the prayer language:

> Pursue love, and earnestly desire the spiritual gifts, especially that you may prophesy. For one who speaks in a tongue speaks not to men but to God; for no one understands him, but he utters mysteries in the Spirit. On the other hand, the one who prophesies speaks to people for their up-building and encouragement and consolation. The one who speaks in a tongue builds up himself, but the one who prophesies builds up the church. Now I want you all to speak in tongues, but even more to prophesy. The one who prophesies is greater than the one who speaks in tongues, unless someone interprets, so that the church may be built up. (*1 Cor. 14:1*–5, ESV)

As believers, we have the opportunity to tap into our secret prayer language that God gives to His children. By using your own prayer language, you're allowing your spirit man within you to intercede on your behalf, directly to God. Your spirit man knows exactly what to pray and will pray perfectly to our God. Many times we run out of words of adoration with which to worship God. We want to pray but get bogged down for lack of words to properly express what is in our hearts. When we let the Spirit pray through us in His limitless language, our spirits can pray for hours and pray perfectly. Many times we have no clue what we are praying, but God knows.

I wanted everything that God had for me. I was hungry for more of Him. I felt tongue-tied when she asked if that was something I had asked God for. I could only stare at her blankly and that made her chuckle. She took my hands in hers and told me that God had already given me my prayer language; I just had to let my carnal mind and natural understanding go. I was never going to understand it with my intellect. She said that when some people first receive the gift, a fully articulate language flows right out of them. For others, it begins intentionally. For example, all a baby can do is make vocal sounds, then later, syllables begin to form, "dada, mama." It is the same with the language of the Spirit. For some, it takes time to fully develop the language. So many times we have a closed-minded approach to what the language of the Spirit should sound like, but I have learned that even among the 6,500 known languages of our planet, there are many that defy the norm: the bush people of the Kalahari communicate with little more than the clicking of their tongues; a tribe in New Zealand communicate with what to the untrained ear sounds like, "Ni ni ni ni ni," with a vast range of inflections.

I had expected the spirit language to burst out of me like a river—a full-sounding language that came of its own accord, so I had never taken the first step. That night I did. I started with a few syllables, then before I knew it, I became comfortable, and the spirit language flowed out of me. Every day I spend time worshipping God and praying to Him in the Spirit.

In September of 2012, I had another encounter with the supernatural realm. I awakened in the middle of the night to use the bathroom, then I felt my way back to the bed in the dark because I was too lazy to turn on the lights.

After crawling into my warm bed, I was waiting for sleep to overtake me when I heard a downpour of rain outside. I could hear the rain falling onto the roof and running down the sides of the house. I lay there unmoving, not making a sound as I listened to the big drops cascading off the roof and splashing onto solid ground.

There were two problems with this situation. One, it was not raining outside; I was sure of it. Two, the sounds were distant, yet at the same time, I knew it was my house that was being rained on even though it sounded far away. At one point, I even held my breath to make sure I was hearing correctly. Just as calmly as it began, it gradually stopped. This experience lasted about forty-five seconds. When it stopped, I jumped out of bed and ran to the window. Nothing. Not a drop of rain outside. But I was sure of what I had heard.

I immediately remembered a sermon I heard from a TV pastor. He said, "When you hear rain in the supernatural but see drought in the natural, don't worry. The rain is falling in the supernatural and will fall in the natural in God's timing."

This was so encouraging. God was stirring up things in my life and cleansing me, making me new, anointing me for something greater. The plans and purposes He has for me are so much bigger than what I could ever hope for. Through the supernatural rain, He was reminding me that His plan is unfolding, and although my circumstances show that things may not be going the way I planned, it's working out for His good and for my good. God will blow our minds and propel us forward if we are obedient to Him.

I'm far from perfect, but I keep Him at the center of my life. Every time a door opens, I am reminded of what I told Him, "Show me how far you're willing to take me!"

Freedom

We can't be full of God if we are full of ourselves

Draw near to God, and he will draw near to you. Cleanse your hands, you sinners, and purify your hearts, you double-minded. (James 4:8)

When God delivered me from homosexuality, it was as if another layer of blindness fell from my eyes and a new understanding was revealed. Although I accepted Christ into my heart in 2008, I didn't understand that I was still living for myself, not God. I was blinded as to how strong Satan's grip on my life still was. The best way to explain it is by using a very popular analogy that I first heard in a sermon by Pastor Andy Stanley: *Fan vs. Follower.*

Whatever your favorite sport is, imagine your being in the bleachers along with thousands of other screaming die- hard fans. What are the characteristics of diehard fans? Fans wear the jerseys and paint their faces so everyone knows whose side they are on. They talk trash to everyone who belittles their team, and they are usually always rowdy. They try to attend games as often as possible. They know a lot about the players (whatever is displayed through media). When the season is over, fans don't think much about the sport. Certainly not like players do.

Now what are the characteristics of actual players on the team? They put in hard work every day of the off-season, preparing themselves for the next season's games. They endure stress, whether it is because of false information blared by the media, the paparazzi watching their every move, or the pressures to be better than the prior season. All eyes are on them. Players live, breathe, and eat their sport. It is their livelihood, and everything rises and falls on their dedication and endurance.

When it comes to Christianity, are you a fan or a follower? Do you represent Christianity poorly? Are you claiming a relationship with Christ yet have spent no time developing that relationship since the day you got saved? Is your life showing little or no evidence of Christ Himself living through you? Or are you developing your relationship with God by spending time with Him, through praying and devouring the Word of God? Are you going to church, hanging around other Christ followers, and searching the Scriptures for truth?

There are too many who claim to be Christian, yet they live and look like the world (Satan's kingdom). If you were to examine their lives to compare them with the Bible, you would find little or no resemblances. This pseudo Christianity does nothing but confuse those who have not yet made a decision to accept Christ as their Savior, as well as those struggling Christians who are feeling God's tug on their lives.

We cannot expect complete freedom when we are full of

ourselves and have no room for God to speak to us or download His truths into us. It is only when we relinquish our understanding and our ways, and begin to seek Him that the blinders will come off our eyes, and we will experience complete freedom.

We need to understand that in the Christian walk, we are not without pain. Many people didn't understand why I would hurt or become depressed if my decision to leave homosexuality was the right thing to do. They often said something like, "If God loves you and wants the best for you, then why are you so miserable? He doesn't seem like a loving God to me."

The pain we experience while walking with Christ is different from the pain we experience when we choose to walk alone, apart from Christ. When we walk alone, doing things our way, we never find complete wholeness in our lives. Instead, we are often left feeling empty, hurt, and lonely. We become experts at covering up our hurts with smiles and laughter or alcohol and drugs, or some other facade to mask the empty feelings.

When we choose to walk with Christ, we will experience pain in the process of growing. Growing pains hurt. I've cried myself to sleep as God seemingly took away every friend I had, leaving me to talk and express my hurts to only Him. Currently in my fifth year of singleness, many times I have experienced the pain of loneliness.

God's correction is often painful, as He allows us to learn by falling flat on our faces until we get it right. As we wait for God to do what He said He will do in our lives, the waiting itself is sometime painful. But I would *never* exchange the pain of walking with the Lord for anything in this world.

After fully surrendering my life to God, I began applying what I had been learning through the years in church, through online sermons, and through reading the Bible. As I focused more on God, believing what the Bible says about me, and focused less on my flesh and natural senses (what I see and feel), I began to see changes in my life. By placing my hope solely in God (relinquishing my way of doing life) and being totally ready, although scared, to do things His way, the turnaround has been amazing. God continues to fill every hole in my life that was created because of bad choices, hurts, and disappointments in my past. I no longer try to drown my sorrows or fill those empty spaces inside me with sex, relationships, alcohol, etc.

I've learned to take every thought captive to the obedience God. What does this look like you wonder? "For the weapons of our warfare *are not* weapons of the world but are mighty in God for pulling down strongholds, casting down arguments and every high thing that exalts itself against the knowledge of God, bringing every thought into captivity to the obedience of Christ" (2 Cor. 10:4–5, NKJV).

When I take every thought captive to the obedience of God, I literally take every thought that does not line up with the Word of God and rebuke it in the name of Jesus. I then speak what the Word of God says pertaining to that area. In doing so, I am casting down the thoughts that attempt to exalt themselves above the knowledge of God (the Bible). By doing this, I am working the process of renewing my mind. (Romans 12:2 ESV, "Do not be conformed to this world, but be transformed by the renewal of your mind...")

As a believer and follower of Christ, when I have an inappropriate thought about a past relationship or a sexual thought about a woman, I immediately say something on the order of, "I rebuke that thought in the name of Jesus. Father God, Your Word says that I am a new creation in Christ Jesus and the old has passed away (2 Cor. 5:17). I thank You that Your Word is true and that I can walk in victory against any schemes of the enemy."

Over the years I have developed this type of prayer life. The more I rebuked every negative thought, the less often they came. The more I entertained those negative thoughts, the more frequently they came. In order to know if we are entertaining a negative thought, we have to read the Bible and spend time with God in prayer. If the thoughts lead me to sin, I should not entertain them.

Spiritual Warfare

No matter what, don't give up!

> Be sober-minded; be watchful. Your adversary the
> devil prowls around like a roaring lion, seeking
> someone to devour. (1 Pet. 5:8 ESV)

If you are living a life outside of God's will, Satan has no real reason to mess with you unless he knows that God is calling you. When you become a believer in Christ, however, Satan will go to any length to try to bring you back into his kingdom. His attacks are more intense with some people than with others, but the moment we receive Christ into our hearts, Satan goes to work to "kill, steal, and destroy" (John 10:10).

The truth is, if Satan can scare you into thinking that this whole "following God" thing is way too much to deal with, he wins in your life. I see so many people walk away from God when the enemy begins to bombard them.

Even after God delivered me from homosexuality, it was difficult at times when my thoughts wandered to Aaliyah or to my little Princess. At the thought of them, my mind would zero in on them for what seemed like five or ten minutes—thinking about how perfect they were or how I missed them like crazy. I did this often during the first few years.

I also noticed that my eyes began lustfully wandering to women I saw as I ran errands around town or even while I attended church services. My mind began taking every attractive woman directly to bed. At that point, I wondered, *Is deliverance only temporary?*

God answered me in a way that scared me straight. He knew that I was hardheaded and needed to be talked to sternly. One night, as I was sleeping, He gave me a dream. In my dream, a friend and I walked into a classroom full of students. We remained unnoticed as the students carried on a debate/discussion about the Muslim faith. The Muslim believers in the classroom were making several points that the non-Muslims thought to be interesting, even though it went against their own faith. As we stood in the back of the classroom observing, I sensed, in the natural (real-time here on earth) but saw in the spiritual realm, a demonic spirit on the left side of my bed, about four feet away in between the walls, awaiting permission. Within the dream, the demonic spirit was a black shadow that was on the left side of me there in the classroom but probably ten feet away and here, too, waiting for permission.

As the students continued talking amongst themselves, I knew that if I thought the thought I was about to think, I would be giving that demonic spirit permission into my life. Being the stubborn woman I am, I did what I wanted. One of the students made a statement about the Muslim faith, and I thought to myself (in the dream), *Hmm, that IS interesting.*

The moment I allowed that thought into my heart, the demonic spirit (in the natural) came through the wall and glided from near the top left corner of my bed, toward the bottom left corner. As I lay in my dream state, paralyzed, unable to speak or move, yet knowing what is going on in the natural, I tried my best to say "Jesus." As I fought for words, and before I could get His name out, I felt something like a wave go through my body that came from the demonic spirit. Right after that happened, I got the name of "Jesus" out of my mouth. Immediately the paralysis broke, and I was able to move.

Science calls experiences similar to mine "sleep paralysis" and says that it's harmless. This is not true. It's demonic, and those who have encountered these types of activities are experiencing things in the spiritual realm. That in itself is a topic for another time.

God explained through this dream that our thoughts, left unchecked, create strongholds that eventually lead to active disobedience to God. Unchecked, wrong thinking produces sin, giving Satan access into our lives. Sin left unchecked can change our thinking from being God-focused to self- focused. Inevitably, if we remain self-focused, we will slip away from God. God let me know immediately that if I continued to play with fire, I was going to get burned.

10 Freedom from Homosexuality

J ust because God freed me from the bondage of homosexuality
does not mean that the journey has been easy or that it's
over. Before God opened my eyes, I couldn't understand how
someone could claim they were delivered, yet in the same breath,
state that they had to somehow live a life of choosing to ignore their
feelings and proclivity toward the same sex. That made no sense to
me, and if that were the case, I didn't want that kind of freedom. I
thought, *What kind of God would allow someone to suffer through life,
pre*tending to be someone they're not?

I would like to take a few moments to clarify this misconception.

What does it mean to be delivered? The word *deliverance* as
defined by the dictionary is "the action of being rescued or set free."
Does deliverance mean that the sin you struggle with will vanish
and cease to be a problem? Yes and no. In my personal experience,
when I have asked God to set me free from things that I struggled
with all my life, some of the turnarounds were almost immediate
while others have been a process.

When God delivers someone from a stronghold or sin, the chains
that have them bound and blinded from God's truth are immediately
broken. The person is no longer a slave to that sin. But once those

chains are broken, what happens next? Some people, not knowing how to walk away from the chains, pick them up again because it's what they're used to. They don't know how to operate in life without them, no matter how messed up going backward might be. You may see a person fall back into whatever traps the devil had them in—abusive relationship, pornography, adultery, alcohol abuse, homosexuality, etc. Why?

When walking with God, we are not without trials, struggles, temptations, and tribulation. Jesus said in John 16:33 (NKJV), "These things I have spoken to you, that in me you may have peace. In the world *you will have tribulation*; but be of good cheer, I have overcome the world."

Some think that after deciding to follow Christ, everything is supposed to be a walk in the park. That is not the case. With or without God, we will have ups and downs, good times and bad. But when following God, the bad times are not the same as the bad times we go through without God. Without God, there is a void and sense of hopelessness or confusion. But with God, no matter if our fleshly feelings overwhelm us, there is a deep-seated knowledge and understanding that God knows best and has things under control. Whether we allow God to direct us during these difficult times, or we become frustrated and do what we think is best, is up to us. When life gets difficult, many fall back into their old ways of doing things, while others relentlessly push forward, knowing that these attacks are only Satan trying to take them off course. God wants us to relentlessly push forward, regardless of what comes against us.

When Jesus encountered the adulterous woman, what did He say to her?

The teachers of the law and the Pharisees brought in a woman caught in adultery. They made her stand before the group and said to Jesus, "Teacher, this woman was caught in the act of adultery. In the Law, Moses commanded us to stone such women. Now what do You say?" They were using this question as a trap, in order to have a basis for accusing Him. But

Jesus bent down and started to write on the ground with His finger. When they kept on questioning Him, He straightened up and said to them, "If any one of you is without sin, let him be the first to throw a stone at her." Again He stooped down and wrote on the ground. At this, those who heard began to go away one at a time, the older ones first, until only Jesus was left, with the woman still standing there. Jesus straightened up and asked her, "Woman, where are they? Has no one condemned you?" "No one, sir," she said. "Then neither do I condemn you," Jesus declared. "Go now and leave your life of sin." (John 8:3–11, NIV)

Jesus told her to go and leave her life of sin. In other words, Jesus extended mercy, but in return, required holiness. God did His part, now she has to do her part by walking diligently in her newfound freedom in Christ. Jesus knew that she was not perfect then and that she was not going to be perfect later. He simply had mercy on her, loved her, forgave her, and asked her to leave her life of sin. Following and listening to God, while blocking out the world's haters and the world's opinions, can be difficult. People either push through or give up. But God will make a way for us through it all if we allow Him to.

When it comes to homosexuality, God will tug on a person to make some changes. One of the first changes God usually asks is, choose different people to hang around. This helped me tremendously. And over time, when I was strong enough, I was able to see and separate healthy relationships from toxic ones.

"Do not be deceived: 'Bad company ruins good morals'" (1 Cor. 15:33, ESV).

When I asked God to help me quit smoking and drinking alcohol, the turnaround was almost immediate when it came to quitting cigarettes. Quitting alcohol has been a process. Regardless of who is around me, I have *no* desire to smoke cigarettes, but if I am around people who are drinking, I struggle with the desire to drink. Although God set me free from it, at times it is a battle in my flesh to say no. For most individuals, leaving homosexuality is a process. God *can* set a person free from any sin, but we live in a fallen world where sin, temptations, and Satan run rampant. With homosexuality, I have learned through the dream mentioned in the previous chapter that my thoughts have power. Yes, God delivers us, but it's our job to claim the deliverance and walk it out in our day-to-day lives.

The more we take inappropriate thoughts captive to the obedience of Christ, and speak God's truths over our lives, the easier it gets, and lustful thoughts of people of the same sex slowly dwindle away. But if we allow those thoughts to linger in our minds, and start entertaining them, we start a downward spiral that will take us right back into the strongholds from which we have been delivered.

Entertaining lust-filled thoughts has a snowball effect on our lives. If we fuel inappropriate thoughts, we not only hinder the process toward freedom, but also lose ground that we have gained. For instance, if I see an attractive woman walk by, my mind may automatically create an initial lustful thought about her. What I do with that thought is key. I can play with it, taking her to bed in my mind, or I can take that thought captive into the obedience of Christ, by saying something such as, "God, thank you for my beautiful sister that you placed here on this earth to fulfill her God-given purpose. Give her a heart after You, and bless everything she does."

On the other hand, if I choose to play with the thought, I will only sink deeper into Satan's trap, possibly, or eventually acting upon the thought. Thoughts left uncontrolled create chaos and give Satan the opportunity to steal the freedom God has given me. The longer I walk in my deliverance, the less frequently these kinds of thoughts come. A woman that I once would have drooled over can walk by, and I will not have a sexual thought about her. I might think, *Dang, those shoes are hot!* But that is as far as my mind takes it.

God revealed to me that the problem was not with His ability to deliver me from homosexuality, but the problem was in my thought life as well as in my relationship with Him. If I am not developing my relationship with Him, I won't get very far. God gives all of us free will. If we choose, we are free to sin and ignore Him. But if we truly have a relationship with God, we will believe and follow Him because we trust Him in spite of not knowing what the future holds. When we have walls up between God and us because we fear being let down or hurt by Him, we will never experience true freedom.

So many times we see God in the same way as we see our earthly fathers or mothers. If our parents were never around or were abusive or unloving, we may have a natural tendency to feel fearful that God will at some point choose not to love us. Perhaps we feel that He will be disappointed with us, and take something away from our lives that we deeply desire.

I lived a life with the Great Wall of China between God and me. As I was growing up, my father was very strict, and I always felt that I needed to live up to his standards of achievements in order to receive praise and love from him. If I got a good grade, did something praiseworthy, or my clothing and physical appearance was up to par, I felt loved by him. But if these criteria were not met, I felt unloved and rejected. My mother, on the other hand, would give her love and take it away so often that I developed trust issues. When I finally came to God, I looked back and saw how I had perceived God to be just like my parents. I had been fearful that God would not love me for who I was because I was nothing like those "perfect Christians" who seemed to receive blessing after blessing. I wondered why God, Who was perfect and supreme, would waste time, energy, and love on someone like me. I didn't want to go "all in" for God, only to experience disappointment from Him. If there was one disappointment I didn't want, it was disappointment from God. I couldn't take that chance, so I relied on myself.

We cannot look at God in the same manner as we look at people because God is not like people. He is an all-powerful Supreme Being, perfect in every way. If we seek Him, He will reveal Himself to us and love us right where we are. Gay, straight, alcoholic, murderer, or whatever, He simply wants to love us. I always tell people who desire to leave homosexuality: "Don't worry about trying to change your same-sex attractions on your own. That's not your job. Focus on developing your relationship with God and allow Him to love you. He will handle the rest!"

11 Spiritual Warfare

D emons wait in the background for permission to invade our lives. Unknowingly, we give them that permission all the time as we entertain our minds and hearts with things that stimulate our sinful nature. Satan is extremely patient. Slowly he crafts schemes and traps that he's placed not only in our individual lives, but also within the world, so that he can integrate and weave his agenda into mankind. I have had to stop watching many TV shows and movies because their themes are sexual or anti-Christ in nature. Many cartoons are also questionable because of the way they subtlety place witchcraft, things relating to the demonic, Satan worship, etc., into their seemingly innocent and kid-friendly programs. Even in one of the most popular bookstores in the U.S., I've noticed that the books on witchcraft, tarot cards, and Satanism are placed strategically next to the children's section. Why? The best way to change a mind is to mold it from the beginning.

Many feel that they are in control of what negatively or positively affects them, but this is not true.

For instance, if we are non-believers, and we watch scary, demonic movies, we begin to develop awareness, carefully crafted by the writers of these scripts, of the nature of the supernatural or demonic realm and how it operates, if it exists. Now if a Christ follower were to talk to a non believer about heaven, hell, the supernatural, etc., they would already have a preconceived notion that these things could not possibly exist. This is solely the stuff of fiction—something man has concocted for movies that are entertaining in a dark way but couldn't possibly be real because they sound ridiculous or far-fetched. Any understanding that a person would try to receive from the believer would have to first break through preconceived misconceptions before someone can begin to understand the truth of the spirit realm.

The Bible tells us to guard our hearts and minds, but we are so used to being deeply integrated with the world and being our own gods that we ignore the one true God. We tend to think that Satan cannot influence us if we choose to ignore him and that we are in charge of what happens in our lives, as well as in charge of our eternal destiny. Trust me. We are not that smart, and we are not that powerful. We cannot outsmart Satan on our own or defeat him except through the power of Jesus Christ.

Satan is intelligent, cunning, and deceitful. There are so many things that Satan uses to infuse his characteristics into us and into our lives. Satan's original name given by God was Lucifer, which means "morning star" or "shiny one." He is beautiful in appearance and may seem kind and loving at first. Satan once lived in heaven and was one of God's top ranking angels. Unfortunately, Satan became jealous of God, was filled with pride, and desired to take God's position, which resulted in God expelling Satan from heaven, and hell became Satan's eternal home.

Since Satan was cast down from heaven to Earth, his devoted purpose is to make sure that he prevents as many people as possible from entering heaven's gates because he knows that it grieves the heart of God when souls are eternally lost. Satan started his trickery and deceit with Adam and Eve and continues those same tactics day in and day out. After his fall, Lucifer became known as Satan, which means adversary. He has many other names, which portray his evil nature: Abaddon (destruction); Beelzebub (ruler of demons); accuser, adversary, anti-Christ, devil, father-of- lies, god-of-this-world.

Too many times, people involve themselves in unbiblical religious ideas, situations, or activities without having any idea that Satan's hand is right in the middle of them. These things may appear innocent in nature, but deceit is Satan's specialty. If he can get us to unknowingly follow him, he wins, and we are chained to him until we give our lives to God.

Many people believe that Satan can't possibly be working in their lives because their lives do not appear to be bad or evil. They're seemingly happy; they have good jobs, money, family, etc. They are living the American dream.

The truth is, if we don't have Christ at the center of our lives, all of the riches and happiness on this earth mean nothing. Satan will offer riches to us just as he offered them to Jesus in the wilderness. What Satan doesn't tell us is that what comes along with surface-level happiness is death. Jesus didn't take Satan's bait and neither should we. Hell, and nothing but hell, awaits those who reject and refuse to follow Christ.

I have a choice. Will I endure persecution while here on Earth for a few years because I serve Jesus, or will I endure an eternity of indescribable torment in hell because I rejected Him? I choose Jesus. Now.

How does Satan infuse his agenda into the world? In what ways have we unknowingly allowed Satan into our hearts and minds? Here are a few traps into which many have fallen:

- Astrology/ Horoscopes
- Witchcraft/ Sorcery/ Black or white magic/ Levitation/ Yoga (religion)/ Transcendental meditation/ Hypnosis
- Violent video games
- All other religions besides Christianity/Free Masonry/ Religions that invoke the name of Christ but do not present Him as the only way to God
- Bloody Mary/ Light-as-a-Feather/ Ouija board
- Objects of worship (people, idols, saints)

When I first heard Christians speak of these things and calling them "gateways for the enemy to come into our lives," I thought they were crazy. But as I grow in Christ, I now have a better understanding of the reality of these gateways. The Bible tells us,

> For we are not fighting against people made of flesh
> and blood, but against persons without bodies—the
> evil rulers of the unseen world, those mighty satanic
> beings and great evil princes of darkness who rule
> this world; and against huge numbers of wicked
> spirits in the spirit world. (Eph. 6:12, TLB)

The battlefield is in the mind, in the spiritual realm, and also in the natural. I've had to renounce many things that I had been involved in throughout my life such as: playing childhood games that appeared innocent in nature such as, Light-as-a-Feather, Bloody Mary, Ouija Board (occult games). I've renounced horoscopes, hypnosis, cutting (self- mutilation), watching movies that glorify Satan or cause fear and nightmares, as well as participating in religious activities that did not glorify Jesus Christ.

As we renounce these things, demons have no other choice but to leave. Once we have renounced demonic activity, we must fill ourselves with Jesus, otherwise, those demons will come back and bring friends (Luke 11:25). The Bible says that Jesus is light and Satan is darkness. If we are full of light, then there is no room for the darkness of the enemy. But if we tell darkness to leave, but we don't fill ourselves with the light of Christ, darkness *will* come back. I have seen some crazy things over the past few years.

Things that I thought only existed in scary movies. Many people have experienced things that they choose to keep to themselves for fear that others might not understand or be able to help. I have had kids come up to me and share their stories of how they have seen demons or dark shadows walking throughout their houses. Maybe it was an apparition of a small child running from one area of the house to another or a person staring at them at the end of the hall. These things are real, and they are demonic.

I was house sitting for a friend one time while she and her family were out of town for a few days, and as I got settled in the house, I felt uncomfortable but was unsure as to why. That night I got into bed, ready for some much needed sleep. As I began to nod off, I felt what I could only describe as a wave passing over me. I immediately knew it was demonic. It felt cold, unwelcoming, and I could sense hate emanating from it. The wave passed over the top half of my body, from the right to left, as I lay there paralyzed and unable to speak. Throughout the night, each time I started drifting into sleep mode, the wave would pass over me, paralyzing me. Struggling to say "Jesus" from my paralyzed lips, I could feel the demonic presence hovering in the room.

Eventually I forced the mighty name of Jesus out through my lips, and the demonic activity ceased…until I began to fall asleep again. Each time, I would tell the demonic presence to "leave in Jesus' name." After the third or fourth attempt at sleep, I clearly understood that the demon did not want me there. Having to get up early for work the next morning, I packed up my stuff and left the house around midnight and went home.

If we are not completely committed to Christ and are truly following Him, Satan and his demons will laugh as we blindly fight battles that we don't understand. If we are *all in* for Christ, we have the authority to command demons to flee and they must go. "Behold! I have given you authority and power to trample upon serpents and scorpions, and physical and mental strength and ability over all the power that the enemy possesses" (Luke 10:19, amp).

This is not to say that God cannot work in the same manner on behalf of an unbeliever; He can do whatever He wants, and I love that about Him. But eventually, we must decide whose team we want to be on: the winning side or the losing side.

The end of the story has already been written in the Bible. Satan loses. He may wreak havoc here on Earth and try his best to deceive everyone, but God wins the war. The way Satan deceives has not changed from the beginning of time when he deceived Adam and Eve. He constantly tries to trick us into following him.

Satan will use the Bible, twisting it to make it seem ludicrous and get us to sin. Let's take a look at the story of Jesus in the wilderness:

> Then Jesus was led up by the Spirit into the wilderness
> to be tempted by the devil. And when He had fasted
> forty days and forty nights, afterward He was hungry.

109

Now when the tempter came to Him, he said, "If You are the Son of God, command that these stones become bread."

But He answered and said, "It is written, 'Man shall not live by bread alone, but by every word that proceeds from the mouth of God.'"

Then the devil took Him up into the holy city, set Him on the pinnacle of the temple, and said to Him, "If You are the Son of God, throw Yourself down. For it is written: 'He shall give His angels charge over you,' and, 'In their hands they shall bear you up, Lest you dash your foot against a stone.'"

Jesus said to him, "It is written again, 'You shall not tempt the Lord your God.'"

Again, the devil took Him up on an exceedingly high mountain, and showed Him all the kingdoms of the world and their glory. And he said to Him, "All these things I will give You if You will fall down and worship me."

Then Jesus said to him, "Away with you, Satan! For it is written, 'you shall worship the Lord your God, and Him only you shall serve.'"

Then the devil left Him, and behold, angels came and ministered to Him. (Matt. 4:1–11, NKJV)

Before Jesus began His ministry, He was led by the Spirit into the wilderness to be tempted by Satan himself. Satan knew that if He could get Jesus to sin, then Jesus would not have been worthy to die on the cross to redeem man from the bondage of sin. But Jesus was not moved by Satan's trickery. In fact, Jesus used Scripture to combat Satan's lies. Notice how Satan used Scripture to try to confuse and deceive Jesus. But Jesus knew the Scriptures very well. He called Satan out when Satan twisted Scriptures in an attempt to get Jesus to fall into sin. Through this whole encounter, Jesus, our example in life, was showing us how to combat the assaults of Satan.

We must know the Word of God and know it well. If we are well grounded in the Bible, we will know immediately when someone takes verses out of context. Satan is a master at trying to get us to believe his distorted use of the Bible. What Scriptures do you use to justify wrong behavior or thinking? How many times has Satan told you, "It's okay to do this or think that, because the Bible says, 'We know that all things work together for good to those who love God...'" (Rom. 8:28). Some people use Scriptures such as this to justify wrong behavior, thinking, *Because I love God, He will fix it.* Wrong! First of all, the writer of Romans is speaking directly to those individuals who love God. What kind of love are they talking about?

> Do not love the world or the things in the world. If anyone loves the world, the love of the Father is not in him. For all that is in the world—the desires of the flesh and the desires of the eyes and pride of life—is not from the Father but is from the world. And the world is passing away along with its desires, but whoever does the will of God abides forever. (1 John 2:15–17 ESV)

Reading the Bible and fully understanding in context what you're reading is so important. This passage in 1 John describes what loving God looks like and lets the reader know that anything contrary to this type of love is not love for God, but love for the world.

So the question is, do you have this kind of love for the Father? The kind of love where you put God first in everything you do? Romans 8:28 ("We know that all things work together for good to those who love God ...") is talking to those who are consumed with the love of Father God. It is not carte blanche for those who do not follow Him.

Many have fallen into the trap of using Scripture to justify bad behavior. We see it all the time. Satan spent forty days in the wilderness trying to mess with Jesus' mind.

How has Satan messed with people's minds over the years,

twisting the Bible to get them to do things that have brought divisions in our world?

A few examples:

- The Ku Klux Klan
- Holy Wars
- Slavery

All of these were fought in the name of Jesus Christ and Christianity. Christianity repulses many because of the evil done in the world in the name of religion. This is one of Satan's slow cooked plans. If he can get us to fight each other, he doesn't have too much work to do. In Jesus' final prayer in John 17, He said in verse 21: "...that they all may be one; just as You, Father, are in Me and I in You, that they also may be one in Us, so that the world may believe without any doubt that You sent Me." If unity is the defining factor for people to believe that God sent Jesus as Savior, we can understand why Satan works so hard to stir up strife and disunity among Christians.

As smart as people are, they so often choose to reject Christ because of others who portray Him poorly. Natural intelligence, however, should tell us that people are not perfect and people are not to be the defining entities when it comes to Christianity. I had come across a quote on Facebook one day and fell in love with it: "We aren't called to be like other Christians; we are called to be like Christ!"

There is so much negativity in the world, and if I had based my desire to find out if Jesus is real on the "Christianity" others show, I don't think I would have had the opportunity to come to know Jesus as I do now. For the longest time, Christians repulsed me by their actions and their ways of thinking. Until I sought Jesus for myself, I remained with that negative mindset and continued a life that was really not worth living—a life filled with voids that I masked very well.

12 Bridging the Gap

How do we fix the disparity between the LGBTQ community and the church while still holding to our beliefs as Christians? How do we love without wavering? How do we stop the hate toward the LGBTQ community, and vice versa? How do we end the confusion over what the Bible actually says about homosexuality? How do we stop the tactics of the enemy?

There is only one way and that is to let Jesus live His life through us.

Hatred breeds hatred. Love breeds love. The light of God's truth casts out darkness. We shouldn't walk around using our Bibles to condemn others; that is counter-productive. Condemnation is not in our job description as followers of Christ. Remember Jesus' words? "Neither do I condemn you. Go and sin no more" (John 8:11). These are the things God asks of us:

- Mark 16:15–16 (ESV): "And he said to them, 'Go into all the world and proclaim the gospel to the whole creation. Whoever believes and is baptized will be saved, but whoever does not believe will be condemned.'"
- Matthew 28:18–20 (NIV): "Then Jesus came to them and said, 'All authority in heaven and on earth has been given to Me. Therefore go and make disciples of all nations, baptizing them in the name of the Father and of the Son and of the

> **Holy Spirit**, and teaching them to obey everything I have commanded you. And surely I am with you always, to the very end of the age.'"

- 2 Peter 1:5–8 (NIV) (Grow Spiritually): "For this very reason, make every effort to add to your faith goodness; and to goodness, knowledge; and to knowledge, self-control; and to self-control, perseverance; and to perseverance, godliness; and to godliness, mutual affection; and to mutual affection, love. For if you possess these qualities in increasing measure, they will keep you from being ineffective and unproductive in your knowledge of our Lord Jesus Christ..."

- Colossians 3:17 (ESV) (Glorify God): "And whatever you do, in word or deed, do everything in the name of the Lord Jesus, giving thanks to God the Father through him."

One of the biggest problems for too many Christians is that they don't know the Bible. They call themselves Christians. They know a few Scriptures. They create a theology for themselves that picks and chooses what is appealing from the Word of God, while leaving out the unappealing, which they would rather not follow.

God's Word is not a buffet table where one can pick and choose only what tastes good, or is appealing to the eye, while ignoring the very things that are necessary for the health of the soul. Picking and choosing creates chaos. Picking and choosing is what Satan wants us to do.

Recently I studied again, with eyes wide open, the gay theology that I once followed. I compared it to the Bible and am fully convinced that gay theology is nothing more than false doctrine that Satan created to deceive the hearts of man. I'm not going into theological depth pertaining to homosexuality in this book. There are several books available for purchase for individual study that do just that.

What I do want to do is explain as simply as possible, how to approach the issue in the church. How would Jesus confront the issue of homosexuality? He hung out with sinners, and much to the horror of the religious leaders of His day, He even ate with them. But Paul writes to a church in Corinth in a letter, stating,

> But now I am writing you that you must not associate with anyone who calls himself a brother or sister but is sexually immoral or greedy, an idolater or a slanderer, a drunkard or a swindler. With such a man do not even eat. What business is it of mine to judge those outside the church? Are you not to judge those inside? God will judge those outside. "Expel the wicked man from among you." (1 Cor. 5:11–13, NIV)

This passage that Paul writes is directed to the church of God in Corinth that was functioning after the resurrection of Jesus. Apparently there were things going on within the church that began to create division. Paul writes to them to provide clarity on how to deal with these issues. We must first note that Paul is talking to those who call themselves brothers and sisters in Christ, but who don't acknowledge their sinful actions as such and refuse to repent for their sins. Paul goes on to say, "Don't even hang out with these people, they shouldn't even be welcome in our churches." Paul is using wisdom.

We as Christians are called "the body of Christ."

> The body is a unit, though it is made up of many parts; and though all its parts are many, they form one body. So it is with Christ. For we were all baptized by one Spirit into one body—whether Jews or Greeks, slave or free—and we were all given the one Spirit to drink. Now the body is not made up of one part but of many. (1 Cor. 12:12–14, NIV)

Since we are the body of Christ, comprised of millions of people, joined together by one God, what do we do if one part of our body becomes infected? If you woke up one morning and noticed that something was wrong within your body, you would go to a doctor. Why? Because an infection left untreated will spread and infect the whole body. If our whole body is infected, we could die. When we as Christians allow Satan to infect the body of Christ (His sons and daughters—the church), nothing but death is sure to come if left untreated. It is our job to treat the infection so it is eradicated and the body heals.

Paul also tells the church, "It's not my business to correct people who are not Christians. It is, however, our jobs to correct those inside of the church" (1 Cor. 5:12).

When I visited his church in Alpharetta, Georgia, I heard Andy Stanley say, "We are to judge the believin', not the heathen." This is exactly what Paul is saying in 1 Corinthians chapter 5. As Christians, it is our job to make sure that we are living right. We all will, at one time or another, sin and make mistakes. No one in the church is perfect. But when we stumble, we should quickly make an effort to get back up again.

Do we always put this into practice? I know that I don't. But I am grateful that God placed me in such a loving church with individuals who are patient, understanding, and forgiving like Jesus. I know they will work with me to get me back into right relationship with God and His body of believers.

Are you harshly correcting your brothers and sisters in Christ when they stray from the Word of God, threatening to kick them out without extending to them the grace that God has extended to you time and time again? Or are you compassionate toward them, allowing the Holy Spirit to work through you, seeing through the eyes of Jesus the heartache, pain, the stronghold, and confusion they are experiencing.

When it comes to homosexuality and many other sins, it is not an overnight change. It's a process. We must have patience with people from the LGBTQ community who attend our churches. We must remember why the church exists in the first place: to bring the lost to Christ. We should never treat a person poorly because they simply sin differently from us.

I have seen people become overly invested in someone else's walk toward freedom. When we become overly invested, we tend to lash out when the person we are helping backtracks or walks away from God. It isn't our job to change people. That's God's job description.

Our job is to give them knowledge of the Word of God and walk with them as they go through the ups and down of life while following God. Yes, it is frustrating to see someone that you've invested time and energy into walk away from God. This is why we pray.

Pray that the seeds you have sown into their lives fall on fertile ground. Pray that someone comes along and waters those sees in their lives and sows more good seed (1 Cor. 3:6–9). Pray that all of the weeds planted by the enemy be uprooted and choked out. Last but not least, ask God to give the increase. Prayer is a powerful tool against the enemy's plans. Pray and let God work. Now, if there are individuals in the church who are in sin and lead others in the church into sin, that needs to be dealt with in another manner. I have been that one in sin, leading others to sin, and I also have seen it done. With no second thought about it, I would set my sights on a girl, and just like Satan, begin a well-thought-out plan to make her mine. This type of behavior should never be accepted in the church.

Satan has attempted to distort in the minds of believers what it means to have godly compassion and empathy.

1. Empathy—*the ability to understand and share the feelings of another.*
2. Compassion—*sympathetic pity and concern for the sufferings or misfortunes of* others.

Be kind to one another, tenderhearted, forgiving one another, as God in Christ forgave you. (Eph. 4:32, ESV)

When he went ashore He saw a great crowd, and He had compassion on them, because they were like sheep without a shepherd. And He began to teach them many things. (Mark 6:34, ESV)

Godly compassion and empathy does not mean we accept sin. It simply allows us to extend God's grace, mercy, and love to broken people.

Jessica A. Newsome

As I said before, Satan will attempt to get us to follow him any way he can. If he can get us to think that we are following our own intellectual ideas, he wins. Through social media, news, LGBTQ-affirming documentaries and movies, etc., he attempts to twist the compassion and empathy of God in our minds and hearts.

Example:

If we look at the media, we see heartfelt stories and moving testimonies of individuals who can't help who they are and who just want to be loved and treated fairly. We hear stories of people who have been treated horribly by the church and disowned by their own families committing suicide because they can't change their sexual orientation or deliver themselves from controlling sins.

Satan whispers to you, "Doesn't God say to love your neighbor? Do not judge? All have sinned and fallen short! Surely God doesn't make mistakes."

This sounds like Satan's line that he used with Jesus in the wilderness, doesn't it?

If you don't have an understanding of the Word of God, you could easily obtain the mindset of "This has to be okay with God." Or maybe you might take the approach of not taking a side and leaving it up to God to judge a person. Both of these types of Christians usually call what they do, "loving the individual, while letting God work in the person's life." For these Christians, I pose a question.

If there is a hell (and there is) where people will spend all of eternity, unless someone tells them what they are doing is against God's law, explaining to them God's saving grace, would you be bold enough to tell them? Would this not be considered love? Ignoring them and their sins and choosing to not to warn them, would that not be considered a form of hate? If we are consumed with self, which is a mark of Satan's kingdom, then no, we wouldn't exert any effort to warn them. But if we truly have the love of Christ, we will gladly and gracefully guide them to Christ.

Have you ever been in a situation where you told someone that you loved, that the way they were living was not God's best for their lives and kindly guided them to the loving and forgiving Christ? If you have, then why can't God reach out to the homosexual through you, as you gently and kindly show them what God's Word says, praying for them, and believing God with them for transformation in their lives. You don't have to Bible-bash them to get this done, just love and allow God to open the door for conversation where you can speak life into them. God loves the homosexual just as much as the alcoholic, the murderer, the liar, the swindler, the thief, and the adulterous husband or wife.

CONCLUSION

The world we live in will always change, but the Word of God will forever remain the same. Without a relationship with Jesus Christ, we will always be searching for something to make us whole or complete. We may try to find that something in one of the numerous religions of the world or search for it in a higher power. We long to know the purpose of life or for the reason for human existence.

These kinds of thoughts and questions will plague our minds throughout life's journey if we don't have a genuine relationship with Jesus Christ. There is a part of us that *must* believe in something. Even having a theory that a person can believe in nothing is, in itself, believing in something.

Over time, constantly trying to find things to fill the emptiness within our souls becomes exhausting. Outside of Jesus, anything that we embrace will provide only temporary satisfaction.

We are created with a desire to know God (Psalm 84:2), but not the god we've fashioned in our minds. That is nothing but an unfulfilling cocktail of "all the things we can think of that are good." Only the living God Who created the universe and everything in it—the God of the Bible will satisfy the longing in our souls. God, the Heavenly Father, knows us to our core, counts every hair on our heads, and knows the reason for every tear. (See Matthew 10:29–31 and Psalm 56:8)

We are created with an innate desire to be in close relationship with the Almighty God Who is always trying to get our attention. Psalm 14:2 ESV says, "The Lord looks down from heaven on the children of man, to see if there are any who understand, who seek after God."

121

He is pursuing you at this moment, so much so, that the poet Francis Thompson called God the Hound of Heaven. When a hound (a breed of hunting dog) zeros in on a scent, he will stop for nothing until he catches what he is pursuing. God does not give up on us. He pursues us because He knows that only when we are in right relationship with Him will we be complete, fulfilled, and totally satisfied.

He wants *you* to know Him. Even as you read this, you may be feeling the very tug of God that I described in chapter 8. If God is calling you to Him, don't delay. He loves you to the moon and back. Maybe you have never received Christ as your personal Lord and Savior, or maybe you have, but you've fallen away, and you want to get back into close relationship with your loving God. The good news is that it's not too late! You can, right now, receive Christ into your heart or renew your relationship with Him.

The Bible says in Romans 10:9–10 (ISV), "If you declare with your mouth that Jesus is Lord, and believe in your heart that God raised Him from the dead, you will be saved. For one believes with his heart and is justified, and declares with his mouth and is saved."

If God is speaking to you, and you want to receive Jesus into your hearts, read the following prayer aloud. The moment you do, Christ will forgive you of all your sins, become your personal Lord and Savior, and heaven will become your eternal home.

"God, I need You in my life and desire to know You. Forgive me of all my sins. I believe that Your Son, Jesus, died on the cross for my sins and rose on the third day, taking the keys of hell and the grave. I declare Jesus as my personal Lord and Savior. Heaven is my eternal home. I am saved. I pray this in Jesus' name, Amen."

> "For I know the plans I have for you," declares the Lord, "plans to prosper you and not to harm you, plans to give you hope and a future. Then you will call on Me and come and pray to Me, and I will listen to you. You will seek Me and find Me when you seek Me with all your heart. I will be found by you,"

declares the Lord, "and will bring you back from captivity." (Jer. 29:11–14, NIV)

Minutes after God delivered me from homosexuality, this Scripture, Jeremiah 29:11–14, came alive in my heart. I believe God is saying the same thing to you. Whether you have given your life to Christ or not, He has a plan for you if you will choose Him. He has a plan that will put you on the path leading to your God-given purpose—a plan that will make you complete and whole, filling every void within you. We must always seek God and never think that we have Him all figured out. The moment we put God in a box, we put a lid on our growth as followers of Christ.

Change does not come overnight. It does not matter what stronghold you're walking out of, Satan will do anything in his power to try to keep you bound to him in the chains of your past or present. Just know that Jesus has triumphed over Satan. Satan is a defeated enemy. If you know the truth, the truth will set you free (John 8:32).

The first step on your journey to freedom is to accept Jesus as your personal Lord and Savior.

The second step is to let God direct you to a church that believes in the whole Bible, a church with Christ followers who live their lives according to the Word of God. There are many churches that speak about Jesus but do not walk in the supernatural authority of Jesus. (See Matt. 28:16–20, Mark 16:17–18.)

The third step is to pay attention to the tugging on your conscience by the Holy Spirit. One of the first tugs of the Holy Spirit will be to watch who you hang around.

It is extremely difficult to move forward when surrounded by people whose mindsets and actions will keep you stuck in the past. God might have to separate you from many people, at least for a while, until you get to a healthy place through the transforming power of the Word of God. The fourth step is to know that this process takes time.

You didn't get yourself into a mess all in one day, so allow God into your heart so He can start the cleanup process from the inside.

When the inside is right, the outside will conform to what has happened internally.

The fifth step is to always remember that God loves you and has your best interest at heart. He sees all that you're going through. If you keep your focus on Him and follow Him, He will lead you on the path of everlasting life.

To the LGBTQ community, I pray that this book has helped you understand what being a follower of Christ truly is. I pray that you have a better understanding of God's endless love for you and His desire for you to be in right relationship with Him.

To the Christian, I pray that you have a deeper understanding of God's love for humanity as well as God's intolerance for sin. I pray you have found insight into the stronghold of homosexuality and have learned how to confront it within the church.

I pray that everyone has a clearer picture of Satan's schemes and tactics to divide the Church and create chaos in the world.

I thank God that He guided me as I wrote the words within these pages because I could not have done it on my own. I truly believe that this unusual love letter is inspired by God to bring healing and freedom to a lost generation of people.

For more information, please visit my nonprofit Web site: www. loveatthecross.com

Blessings,
Jessica

Printed in the United States
By Bookmasters